Painting
Garden Decor

WITH DONNA DEWBERRY

NORTH LIGHT BOOKS

CINCINNATI, OHIO
www.artistsnetwork.com

About the Author

Donna Dewberry is a wife, mother of seven, grandmother of three (soon to be four), daughter, sister, native Floridian and passionate decorative painter. She is also a teacher and author of three other North Light books, *Donna Dewberry's Complete Book of One-Stroke Painting*, *Decorative Murals with Donna Dewberry*, and *Decorative Furniture with Donna Dewberry*. She can be seen on QVC television network selling her One-Stroke technique to hundreds of thousands of viewers. Her artwork is so in demand that it will soon be embellishing a line of clothing and a line of wallpaper.

Donna has her own One-Stroke painting workshop certification classes certifying teachers in the One-Stroke painting technique. She believes that anyone can learn to paint, and she travels the world teaching and encouraging others to experience the joy of creating.

Donna's enthusiasm for painting is shadowed only by her enthusiasm and love for her family and friends. Her true creativity stems from being grounded by the most important things in life, the simple things.

Painting Garden Decor with Donna Dewberry. Copyright © 2002 by Donna Dewberry. Manufactured in China. All rights reserved. The patterns and drawings in this book are for the personal use of the decorative painter. By permission of the author and publisher, they may be either hand-traced or photocopied to make single copies, but under no circumstances may they be resold or republished. It is permissible for the purchaser to paint the designs contained herein and sell them at fairs, bazaars and craft shows. No other part of this book may be reproduced in any form or by any electronic or mechanical means including information storage and retrieval systems without permission in writing from the publisher, except by a reviewer, who may quote brief passages in a review. Published by North Light Books, an imprint of F&W Publications, Inc., 4700 East Galbraith Road, Cincinnati, Ohio 45236. (800) 289-0963. First edition.

Other fine North Light Books are available from your local bookstore or art supply store, or direct from the publisher.

06 05 04 03 02   5 4 3 2 1

Library of Congress Cataloging-in-Publication Data
Dewberry, Donna S.
   Painting garden decor with Donna Dewberry.
     p. cm.
   Includes index.
   ISBN 1-58180-144-0 (pbk. : alk. paper) -- ISBN 1-58180-143-2 (alk. paper)
     1. Painting. 2. Decoration and ornament. 3. Garden ornaments and furniture. 4. Garden tools. I. Title:Painting garden decor. II. Title.

TT385 .D48424 2002
745.7'23--dc21   2001044485

Editor: Gina Rath
Production Coordinator: Mark Griffin
Designer: Joanna Detz
Layout Artist: Linda K. Watts
Photographers: Christine Polomsky and Al Parrish

Metric Conversion Chart

TO CONVERT	TO	MULTIPLY BY
Inches	Centimeters	2.54
Centimeters	Inches	0.4
Feet	Centimeters	30.5
Centimeters	Feet	0.03
Yards	Meters	0.9
Meters	Yards	1.1
Sq. Inches	Sq. Centimeters	6.45
Sq. Centimeters	Sq. Inches	0.16
Sq. Feet	Sq. Meters	0.09
Sq. Meters	Sq. Feet	10.8
Sq. Yards	Sq. Meters	0.8
Sq. Meters	Sq. Yards	1.2
Pounds	Kilograms	0.45
Kilograms	Pounds	2.2
Ounces	Grams	28.4
Grams	Ounces	0.04

A special thank you goes out to Leanne Rosenfeld and to David and Sarah Lewis for graciously opening up their beautiful gardens in which the finished projects were photographed.

Dedication and Acknowledgements

I would like to recognize those who make a difference every day. I know there are many times when they receive little or no recognition, but they still persist. Who are these heroes? They are the mothers, fathers, grandparents, sons, daughters and friends who make up our lives. They are those who, when we were too small to remember, gave us not only the necessities of life, but assisted us in our dreams. They encouraged us in our sometimes unrealistic desires, but nevertheless gave us support. They are those who made us smile and cry, who made time for us, and spent time with us. They are those who, when we won, cheered with us, and when we lost, stood beside us. They are the ones who have remained by our side through the best of times and the worst of times. They are everywhere. They are the people of our lives.

I give thanks to those who have been, and still are, in my life. They have made a difference to me, as I am sure the people in your life have to you.

It is time for me to acknowledge those who have assisted me in the making of this book. So often I feel as though I leave out someone I should have remembered, and I'm sure this time will be no different. So please, in advance, forgive me. I can only imagine how I would ever be able to undertake a project of this magnitude without help.

To all those in my offices and to my family, I give thanks. To all of my friends and associates in the book world I give admiration, for you are truly wonderful people, and without you, none of this would be possible. For those of you who have contributed in any way to this book, I give thanks.

Now for those whom I can remember, "thank you" to my husband Marc and to Maribel, Kathy, and Mike for all the special assistance you gave me.

Table of Contents

Introduction 7

Supplies and
Basic Techniques 8

PROJECT ONE
Stepping-Stones 14

PROJECT TWO
Herb Barrel Stave 22

PROJECT THREE
Mailbox Cutout 28

PROJECT FOUR
White Flowerpot 36

PROJECT FIVE
Watermelon Pots 40

PROJECT SIX
Daisy Mat 46

PROJECT SEVEN
Herb and Insect Pots 52

PROJECT EIGHT
Floral Garden Screen 62

PROJECT NINE
Hydrangea Bench 84

PROJECT TEN
Painted Trash Can 90

PROJECT ELEVEN
Garden Gate 96

PROJECT TWELVE
Wedding Bells
Painted Pots 104

PROJECT THIRTEEN
Birdbath 112

PROJECT FOURTEEN
Gazing Ball
& Watering Can 126

PROJECT FIFTEEN
Topiary Bench 132

Resources 142

Index 143

Introduction

Gardens are becoming an important part of our lives. More and more of us create areas where we can relax, entertain and spend time enjoying our families; all in the privacy of our own backyards. In this book you will learn to use my One-Stroke painting technique to transform ordinary objects into one-of-a-kind garden decor. There are fifteen projects from which you can choose. I have painted on wood, metal, terracotta pots and even vinyl to create fresh and exciting projects that will motivate you to begin livening up your garden today.

My desire for this book, as it is in all of my books, is that it will inspire you to try your hand at painting. Find out just how exciting it is to tap into your own creative ability. I encourage you to pick up a brush and give it a try. Anyone can paint if they just have the information they need to help them get started. This book has all the information you need to take that first step, and I'll be with you each step of the way.

I hope that what you learn from this book will encourage you to step into the world of decorative painting with confidence and pride. Once you feel confident in your painting ability, I urge you to move forward and use my ideas as a jumping-off point to create your own designs. We all want our gardens to reflect our unique personalities. So use these ideas to create the garden decor that reflects your personal style. I hope you will experiment with your newfound talent until painting becomes as exciting a part of your life as it is mine.

So pick up that brush and begin—you will quickly reap the benefits of self-expression. I wish I could be with each of you as you experience the sheer joy of transforming your garden with decorative painting!

Supplies and Basic Techniques

Brushes

Flat Brushes

Painting the one-stroke technique requires the use of flat brushes. The Donna Dewberry One-Stroke brushes are designed with longer bristles and less thickness in the bodies of the brushes to allow for a much sharper chisel edge. A sharp chisel edge is essential to the success of the one-stroke technique, as most of the strokes begin and then end with the use of the chisel edge.

The Donna Dewberry One-Stroke brushes are ready to use from the package. Simply dampen the bristles in water and dry with a paper towel before beginning to paint.

When cleaning these brushes you may use the rake in the bottom of the brush basin; the bristles are not natural and therefore do not have as much of a tendency to break, but be gentle.

Scruffy Brushes

The scruffy brush that I have created is ready to be used straight out of the package. All you have to do is "fluff the scruff" as we say. Remove the brush from the packaging and form the natural bristles into an oval shape by gently pulling on them. Then, twist the bristles in the palm of your hand until you have a nice oval shape. Now you are ready to pounce into paint and begin.

When fluffed, the scruffy brush is used for painting mosses, wisteria, lilacs, certain hair and fur and for faux painting and shading textures. Do not use this brush with water. When cleaning the scruffy brush you need to pounce the bristles into the brush basin. Do not rake them or you will break the natural bristles.

Liner   Script Liner   No. 2 Flat   No. 8 Flat   No. 12 Flat   ¾-inch (19mm) Flat   Medium Scruffy   Small Scruffy

Script Liners

There are two sizes of script liners. The no. 1 (sometimes referred to as the mini) is usually used for small detail work where more control is needed. The no. 2 is used where less control is needed.

The liner brush is used with paint of an "inky" consistency. To acquire this consistency, pour a small amount of paint onto your palette. Dip the liner brush into water, then touch the water to your palette next to the paint. Do this three or four times. Roll your liner brush where the water and paint meet to mix them until you have an inky consistency. Don't mix all of the paint with the water or your mixture will be too thick. Roll the brush out of the inky paint to prevent it from dripping. See page 13 for how to load the liner brush.

Clean these brushes like you do the flat brushes. Once again, be gentle, but clean thoroughly.

Paints and Mediums

Plaid FolkArt Paints

Plaid FolkArt Acrylic Colors are high-quality bottled acrylic paints. Their rich and creamy formulation and long open time make them perfect for decorative painting. They are offered in a wide range of wonderful premixed colors and in gleaming metallic shades.

Plaid FolkArt Artists' Pigments

Artists' Pigments are pure colors that are perfect for mixing your own shades. Their intense colors and creamy consistencies are wonderful for blending, shading and highlighting. Because they're acrylic paints, they're easy to clean up.

Plaid FolkArt Floating Medium

Floating medium allows the paint to stay wetter, thus aiding you with your brushstrokes. When painting the one-stroke techniques, please do not follow the instructions on the bottle. This will make your strokes very muddy.

Instead load your brush as instructed, then dip the tip of the bristles straight down into the puddle of medium. Stroke two or three times on your palette, then you are ready to paint.

1. *Brush basin*
2. *Paper towels*
3. *Rubbing alcohol*
4. *Tracing paper*
5. *Small roller*
6. *Sponge brush*
7. *One-stroke sponges*
8. *Styrofoam plate*
9. *Transfer paper*
10. *Stylus*

Techniques

Double Loading the Brush

1 To double load, dip one corner of your brush first into one color to form a triangle of color on the corner. Make sure the brush is angled when you dip it into the paint.

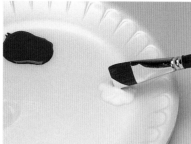

2 Dip the other corner into the second color, forming another triangle. Again, make sure the brush is angled when it goes into the paint.

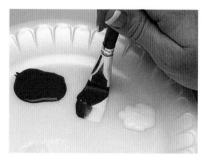

3 Place the loaded brush on your palette and stroke it back, pushing down hard against the palette.

4 Now stroke forward, still putting pressure on the palette to work the paint into the bristles.

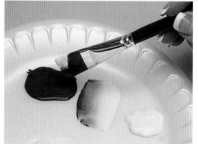

5 Dip each corner again. Repeat the whole process two or three times, from dipping the corners to stroking on the palette.

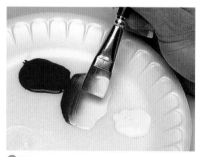

6 When loaded correctly, your brush should be two-thirds full and the area where you stroked on your palette should not be longer than two inches (5cm). If you stroke longer, you'll wipe the paint off of your brush.

7 Once the brush is fully loaded, dip each corner ever so lightly into each paint color one more time (don't stroke on your palette this time). Now you are ready to paint.

8 If the brush begins to feel dry, add floating medium. Dip straight down into the medium. Go back to your palette and work the medium in two or three times. Do not use floating medium more often than every three or four strokes.

hint

When your brush is loaded correctly, your strokes should feel as though they glide. If the bristles split or if the brush grabs or skips as you're painting, you do not have enough paint on your brush.

Side Loading

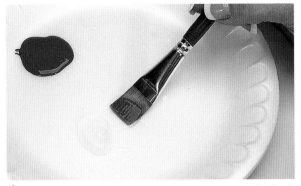

1 To side load a brush with floating medium, stroke back and forth in the floating medium, then stroke back and forth on your palette. Make sure both sides are thoroughly covered with the medium.

2 Side load one edge of your brush into the color desired for stroking. Stroke back and forth on your palette a couple of times.

Multiloading and Starter Strokes

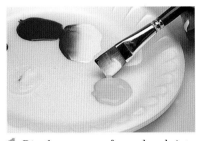

1 Dip the corners of your brush into the first two colors, then ever so lightly add the third and fourth (or more) colors that you want. Add darker colors to the dark side of the brush and lighter colors to the light side of the brush.

2 This is how it looks when a multiloaded brush is stroked.

3 Every time you pick up paint and before you stroke you need to do a starter stroke. A starter stroke is actually three strokes right on top of each other. After the third stroke, continue on with your full stroke.

Transferring the Pattern

Transfer your pattern onto the surface using graphite paper (gray for light surfaces, and white for dark surfaces) and a stylus or ballpoint pen. Insert the graphite paper dark side down under the pattern. Trace the pattern onto the basecoated surface. (Don't trace curlicues; this makes the pattern more difficult to paint.)

Heart-Shaped Leaf

1 Dot a V shape with the chisel edge of your brush. Do your starter stroke, push, then wiggle, pivoting the white edge until you see a seashell shape.

2 Lift and slide evenly to the chisel to end the leaf stroke.

3 Repeat for the other side, starting on the other side of the V. Keep the brush straight up.

Stems

With your brush on the chisel edge, lead with your light color and pull the stem only halfway into the leaf.

Tall Leaf or Ribbon

 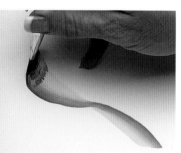 

1 To paint a tall leaf (such as an iris leaf) or a ribbon, double load a large flat brush and begin the stroke on the chisel edge. Keep the brush straight up and down, and push down on the bristles as you stroke.

2 To create a turn in the leaf, keep the brush against the surface and simply turn the brush a bit.

3 To form a loop, don't lift the brush from the surface you are painting. Simply reverse your stroke, then slide up to the chisel edge to end your stroke.

Curlicues

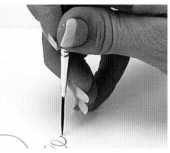

1 Mix up an inky mixture (see page 11) using your liner brush. Make a circular motion at the edge of the puddle.

2 Roll the brush out of the inky puddle. This will help you realize whether the mixture is watery, inky or pasty. You want it to be inky. Rolling also prevents it from dripping.

3 Keep your brush handle straight up and down while painting the curlicues. Brace the brush handle against the second knuckle of your pointer finger, and use your little finger to guide you. Move your whole arm, not just your wrist.

Shadow Leaves

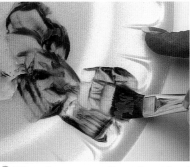

1 Start with a dirty brush (see Hint below right). Wipe excess paint off, then start cleaning the brush in the floating medium. This leaves a dirty puddle of paint in the floating medium with which you can paint.

2 Wipe the excess off on the side of the palette, then start stroking.

3 Stroke your large or small leaves using the dirty puddle color.

Alternating Colors

In this demonstration, I used Berry Wine, Wicker White and Night Sky. Double load your brush with Berry Wine and Wicker White. Paint some of your strokes with this color combination. Go back and dip your brush into Night Sky (on the Berry Wine side), then go back to the Berry Wine to alternate.

hint

A "dirty brush" is usually the last brush you were using. Do not rinse it out—it should still have paint left in it.

Stepping-Stones

Here are three delightful stepping-stones to scatter about your garden path. Even if you (like me) don't have a green thumb, you can still pave your way around any garden and look like a successful gardener.

Each of these stones is actually a 12" x 12" (30cm x 30cm) square of pressure-treated lumber. The top edges on all four sides have been rounded. Each stepping-stone is decorated with a variety of ferns and its own woodland insect.

Once finished, protect your wooden stepping-stones with two or three coats of water-based exterior varnish.

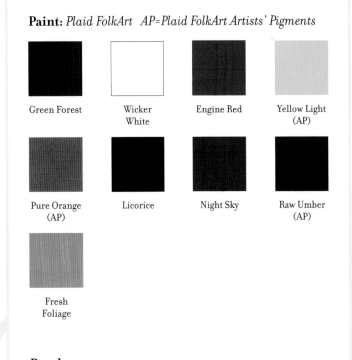

Paint: *Plaid FolkArt AP=Plaid FolkArt Artists' Pigments*

Green Forest	Wicker White	Engine Red	Yellow Light (AP)
Pure Orange (AP)	Licorice	Night Sky	Raw Umber (AP)
Fresh Foliage			

Brushes

no. 12 flat ❖ no. 6 flat ❖ no. 2 script liner

Additional Supplies

graphite paper ❖ tracing paper ❖ stylus ❖ water-based primer ❖ floating medium ❖ water-based exterior varnish

Surface

2" x 12" pressure-treated lumber cut into 12" (30cm) squares, or 12" x 12" (30cm x 30cm) concrete from any hardware store. Seal the concrete with a water-based concrete sealer before basecoating.

Ladybug Stepping-Stone

Butterfly Stepping-Stone

Snail Stepping-Stone

Ferns

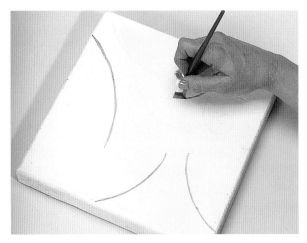

1 Paint all the sides of your stepping-stones with a water-based primer or sealer and allow them to dry. Basecoat with Wicker White, allow to thoroughly dry, then trace on the pattern. Double load your no. 12 flat with Fresh Foliage and Green Forest, then dip into floating medium. Paint all the stems first, using the chisel edge of your brush and leading with the lighter color. Slightly lift the light edge and drag the dark edge. The stems give you the layout or placement for the finished design.

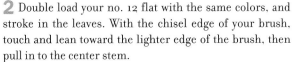

2 Double load your no. 12 flat with the same colors, and stroke in the leaves. With the chisel edge of your brush, touch and lean toward the lighter edge of the brush, then pull in to the center stem.

3 To create this one-stroke leaf, start with your brush on the stem. Push and turn the brush.

4 Then lift to the tip of the leaf.

5 To make longer leaves, push, turn, slide and then lift to the tip. Make these leaves longer as you go down the stem.

Curly Fern

6 Use your no. 2 script liner loaded with inky Green Forest. Hold your liner straight up and down, begin in the center of the curlicue and curl around and back to the edge of the stepping-stone.

7 Load your no. 6 flat with Green Forest, and begin painting one-stroke leaves in the center. If the paint becomes too thick, add a little floating medium. As you go down the stem, make the leaves slightly longer.

8 Go back in with your script liner and inky Green Forest to clean up the stem of the fern.

Ladybug Stepping-Stone

9 Paint all of the ladybugs the same. Use your no. 6 flat loaded with Engine Red to basecoat the ladybug's body.

10 Use the handle of the brush to dot the head with Licorice.

11 Use your no. 2 script liner to paint in the center line. Add six legs, stroking from the body outward.

12 With the handle of your brush, add the dots on the ladybug's body and the dots for the antennae using Licorice.

13 Use your no. 2 script liner to connect the antennae dots to the ladybug's head. After the dots are dry, side load your no. 12 flat with Licorice and floating medium and add a little shading next to the ladybug. Repeat steps 9 through 13 for the other two ladybugs on the stepping-stone.

Butterfly and Snail Stepping-Stones

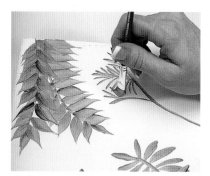

14 All of the fern leaves on this stepping-stone are the same as on the ladybug stone except for one. The leaves of this different fern are thinner and finer than the others. To paint this fern, use the chisel edge of your no. 12 flat double loaded with Fresh Foliage and Green Forest. Dip into floating medium, and paint the leaves ever so lightly with short chisel strokes on the tip of the bristles.

15 All of the butterflies are painted the same. To paint the butterfly, double load your no. 12 flat with Night Sky and Wicker White. Keep Night Sky toward the outside edge of the wings to draw your butterfly shape.

16 Use your no. 6 flat loaded with Night Sky to paint the butterfly body. This is a simple one-stroke touch-push-and-lift to the chisel edge.

17 Use your no. 2 script liner and Night Sky to paint in the antennae. Dot in the spots on the wings with your brush handle and Yellow Light. Use your script liner to add the spots on the wings and to add the detail work. Add some highlights to the body with Wicker White. Shade around one outside edge of the butterfly with Licorice as you did the ladybugs (see step 13).

18 The snail stepping-stone has two slightly different ferns—one with thinner leaves and one with shadow leaves. All of the strokes on the thin leaf fern are pulled from the main stem out to a point. Touch, lean slightly and pull away from the stem on the chisel edge of your no. 6 flat brush double loaded with Fresh Foliage and Forest Green.

19 For the shadow leaf fern, use the same no. 6 flat with your floating medium, then stroke in shadow leaves. Start from the stem and pull out.

Snail

20 Paint all of the snails in the same way. Use your no. 6 flat double loaded with Yellow Light and Pure Orange to stroke in the body of the snail. Lead with the orange, touch, push, pull and lift to the chisel edge.

21 To make the swirl inside the shell, use the same color mixture. Use the orange edge to define the curves in the snail.

22 Use your liner and Pure Orange to further define the edges of the snail. Then paint the antennae.

23 Go back in with Raw Umber to further define these edges. Shade the snail as you did the ladybugs and butterflies.

final step

Protect your stepping-stones with several coats of water-based exterior varnish.

Herb Barrel Stave

With this painted barrel stave, you can bring garden decor into your home and surround yourself with herbs all year long.

This delightful decoration would look great on a screened-in porch or would even fit nicely into a kitchen setting. When I found this barrel stave I knew its interesting shape could enhance all sorts of small areas in and around the home.

Note: This stave may warp if used outside; it should be placed in a protected area, away from inclement weather.

Paint: *Plaid FolkArt   AP=Plaid FolkArt Artists' Pigments*

Thicket

Wicker White

Night Sky

Violet Pansy

Sunflower

Dioxazine Purple (AP)

Brushes

³⁄₄-inch (19mm) flat ❖ no. 12 flat ❖ no. 8 flat
❖ no. 2 script liner

Additional Supplies

graphite paper ❖ tracing paper ❖ stylus ❖ water-based primer or sealer ❖ floating medium ❖ water-based exterior varnish

Surface

wooden barrel stave from Boulder Hill Woodworks

Herbs

This pattern may be hand-traced or photocopied for personal use only. Enlarge first at 200%, then at 167% to bring it up to full size.

Stems and Statice

1 Seal the barrel stave (front and back) with a water-based primer or sealer. Then basecoat with Thicket, allow to thoroughly dry, and trace on the pattern. Multiload your ³/₄-inch (19mm) flat with Wicker White, Sunflower, and Thicket. Using the chisel edge of your brush, lead with the light edge and stroke in the stems of the statice and the main stems.

2 Multiload your no. 12 flat with the same three colors, and stroke in the fine leaves. Pull these leaves out from the stem using short chisel strokes.

3 Dab in the statice blossoms with Violet Pansy and Wicker White using your no. 12 flat.

Stems and Leaves

4 Attach the blossoms to the stems with your no. 12 flat and Sunflower, Thicket, and Wicker White. Chisel downward to the main stem.

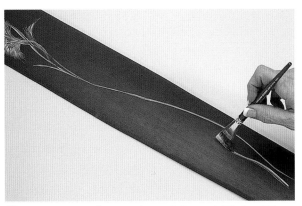

5 Multiload your ¾-inch (19mm) flat with Wicker White, Thicket and a touch of floating medium. Use the chisel edge and pull the stem upward.

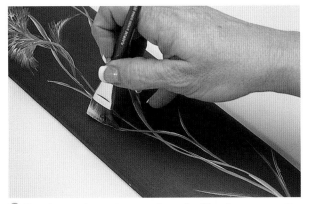

6 Starting on the main stem, branch off and cross over the other stem. This makes the stems look more natural.

7 Stroke in the leaves using your no. 8 flat double loaded with Sunflower and Thicket and a touch of floating medium.

8 Using the chisel edge of your brush, attach the leaves to the plant by pulling a stem from the plant halfway into each leaf.

Flowers and Buds

9 Using your no. 12 flat double loaded with Night Sky and Wicker White, stroke in the petal. Begin with Night Sky on the outside. Start on the chisel edge, push down, wiggle and lift up to the edge again. Flip the brush over once in a while so the Wicker White is on the outside.

10 Still using Night Sky and Wicker White, stroke in the buds. Attach the blossoms to the stem as you did in step 4.

11 Dip your no. 2 script liner into Sunflower and streak through Thicket. Dab in the flower center.

12 Using your no. 12 flat double loaded with Sunflower and Thicket, outline and then fill in the base of the flower.

13 Using the chisel edge of the same brush, crisscross a pattern onto the base.

14 Stroke in the leaves using floating medium with a touch of Sunflower and Thicket. Keep the lighter color to the outside edge. Finish by pulling the stem to the leaf.

Wispy Flower Petals

15 Double load your no. 12 flat with Dioxazine Purple and Wicker White and stroke in the wispy petals using the chisel edge of your brush. Lead with the lighter side.

16 Use the edge of your no. 12 flat loaded with floating medium and Thicket to clean up and shade where the blossom attaches to the stem.

17 Paint the lettering using your no. 2 script liner and an inky mix of Sunflower and Thicket. Pull these strokes downward.

final step

Seal the barrel stave (front and back) with two or three coats of water-based exterior varnish.

Mailbox Cutout

I wanted a way to make my mailbox special without having to ask my husband to do too much. This project fits the bill because it's easy to cut out and just as easy to install. I've painted the cutout with pretty hydrangeas and roses to help me think of spring every day of the year.

Don't rule out painting these same flowers on your mailbox. By simply following the instructions for the flowers, your mailbox can also be transformed into a floral masterpiece.

When painting the hydrangea petals, you will achieve a lovely variety of color by alternating colors on your brush.

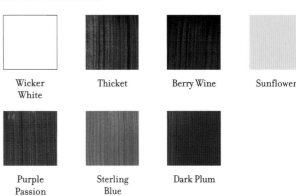

Paint: *Plaid FolkArt*

Wicker White	Thicket	Berry Wine	Sunflower
Purple Passion	Sterling Blue	Dark Plum	

Brushes

³⁄₄-inch (19mm) flat ❖ no. 12 flat ❖ no. 2 script liner ❖ large scruffy

Additional Supplies

graphite paper ❖ tracing paper ❖ stylus ❖ floating medium ❖ water-based exterior varnish

Surface

wooden mailbox cutout by Dewberry Designs

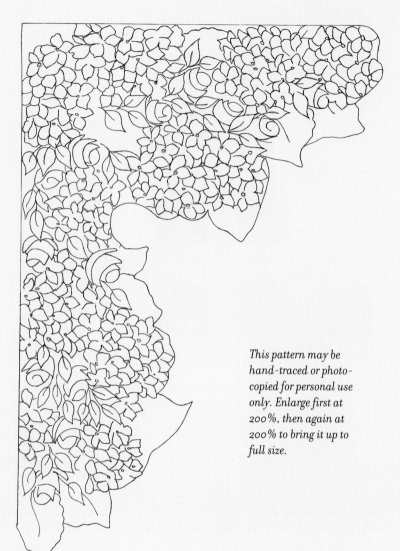

This pattern may be hand-traced or photo-copied for personal use only. Enlarge first at 200%, then again at 200% to bring it up to full size.

Preparation

1 First, prime the wood and allow it to dry. Then basecoat the cutout with two coats of Wicker White. Allow to thoroughly dry, then trace on your pattern.

2 With your fingers, fluff the scruffy brush to prepare for the muted background behind the hydrangeas.

hint

You can paint your floral design first, then cut out the edges of the wood afterward.

Leaves

3 Multiload your ³/₄-inch (19mm) flat with Wicker White, Thicket and some floating medium. While painting the heart-shaped leaves, occasionally pick up some Sunflower (see page 12). Watch the outside (green) edge of the brush as you form the ripply edges. Follow the pattern for placement.

4 Pull a stem halfway into the leaf.

5 With the dark edge of the brush facing up, extend the leaf over the edge of the cutout.

6 Using Wicker White, Thicket, Sunflower, and a little Berry Wine on your large scruffy, pounce in the backgrounds for the hydrangeas. Extend the color over the edges of the wood in places as you did with the leaves.

7 This is how your board looks now.

Rosebuds

8 To begin your rosebuds, stroke up and over from line to line using your ¾-inch (19mm) flat with Wicker White and Berry Wine.

9 Make a **U**-stroke for the front of the bud, from line to line.

10 Make a larger **U**-stroke extending past the bud.

11 On the chisel edge and leaning the white edge of the brush outward, stroke across the front of the bud.

12 Paint the next stroke in the same way, but come from the other direction. Add two or three of these petals.

Hydrangeas

13 For the hydrangea petals, double load your no. 12 flat with Wicker White and Purple Passion. Keep the Wicker White to the outside and stroke up to the tip.

14 Without lifting your brush, lean the bristles in the opposite direction and stroke back down toward the center.

15 Repeat for each petal in the blossom. Each hydrangea blossom has four petals.

16 Alternate colors by picking up Sterling Blue on the Purple Passion side of your brush.

17 Stroke in the petals, keeping the Sterling Blue on the inside and the Wicker White to the outside.

18 Now pick up Berry Wine on the Sterling Blue side of your brush and stroke in pink-toned petals.

19 For more color variation you can flip the brush over and paint the darker color on the outside edge of the petals. Here you see Dark Plum on the Berry Wine side of the brush.

20 Use the tip of your brush handle to dot the centers with Sunflower. To keep it more natural looking, don't dot every single center.

21 Continue filling in the hydrangeas as you cover the pounced-in background areas on your board.

22 Notice that the blossoms of the hydrangeas form a ball shape.

23 Add one-stroke leaves using Wicker White, Sunflower, and Thicket on your no. 12 flat.

24 Using your no. 2 script liner, finish up by adding curlicues with inky Thicket.

final step

Protect your mailbox cutout with several coats of water-based exterior varnish.

White Flowerpot

Covered with wildflowers and baby's breath, this white flower-pot will add a bright touch to your garden. You'll be thrilled with how quick and easy these flowers are to paint.

This pot would make a wonderful hostess gift filled with beautiful flowers or treats, or you could paint several and line your garden path with them as I did. The design for this was my husband's idea, and after I painted several, we placed candles in them to mark our garden path. They looked so beautiful that I took credit!

Note: If you are using your pots for flowers, be sure to seal the inside of the pot (or use a plastic liner). This will prevent moisture from wicking through the terra cotta and popping off the paint.

Paint: *Plaid FolkArt   AP=Plaid FolkArt Artists' Pigments*

| Thicket | Wicker White | Sunflower | Berry Wine |

| Dioxazine Purple (AP) | Yellow Ochre (AP) |

Brushes
¾-inch (19mm) flat ❖ no. 12 flat ❖ no. 6 flat ❖ no. 2 script liner ❖ small scruffy ❖ large scruffy

Additional Supplies
water-based exterior varnish

Surface
8-inch (20cm) terra-cotta pot, from any home goods or craft store or garden center

This pattern may be hand-traced or photocopied for personal use only. Enlarge at 172% to bring it up to full size.

Background and Leaves

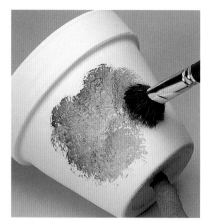

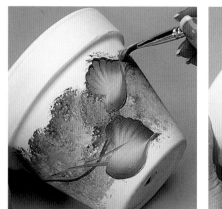

1 *(Left)* Basecoat the terra-cotta pot with Wicker White. Using your large scruffy and Thicket, Sunflower, and Wicker White, pounce in moss background all the way around the pot. Allow it to dry before going on to the next step.

2 *(Right)* Paint in a vine around the pot using your ¾-inch (19mm) flat double loaded with Thicket and Wicker White.

3 *(Left)* Using the same colors, paint in large heart-shaped leaves (see page 12). Pull stems halfway into the leaves.

4 *(Right)* Load your small scruffy with Dioxazine Purple and Wicker White, and pounce in the small purple wildflowers.

Daisies and Baby's Breath

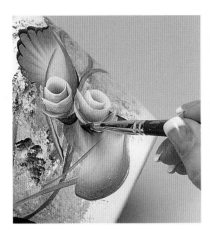

5 *(Left)* Double load your no. 12 flat with Wicker White and Berry Wine, and stroke in the rosebuds, as shown on page 32.

6 *(Right)* Pull stems into the buds. With your no. 12 flat double loaded with Yellow Ochre and Wicker White, paint in the daisy petals, leading with the Yellow Ochre on the chisel edge of your brush. Use your script liner to make the stems of the partial daisies with Thicket. Also use Thicket to dot the daisy centers.

7 *(Left)* Use your small scruffy with Wicker White to add baby's breath. Just one dab per blossom is all you need. Keep the pounces separate so the baby's breath is light and airy. You want the appearance of individual blossoms.

8 *(Right)* Add one-stroke leaves using Thicket on your no. 6 flat. Finish up with curlicues using inky Thicket and your no. 2 script liner.

final step

Protect your pot with several coats of clear varnish. Do not plant in your pot unless you have sealed the inside before painting.

Watermelon Pots

Watermelons and mushrooms were some of the first designs that I ever painted, because I found them easy to shade and I enjoyed the bright colors. I think you too will have fun painting these simple pots.

Use the pots all summer long for garden party settings or for dressing up a lazy summer cookout. Fill them with utensils, or line them with plastic and serve up a pot full of melon slices. The possibilities are limited only by your imagination. The best part is that you will have painted these yourself. So get started and enjoy the painting process!

Note: The smallest pots can become napkin rings. To make them, cut the hole in the bottom of the pot before you paint it (see step 14).

Paint: *Plaid FolkArt   AP=Plaid FolkArt Artists' Pigments*

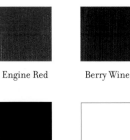

Engine Red	Berry Wine	Green Forest	Yellow Light (AP)

Licorice	Wicker White	Night Sky

Brushes

¾-inch (19 mm) flat ❖ no. 12 flat ❖ no. 6 flat ❖ no. 2 script liner ❖ medium scruffy

Additional Supplies

water-based varnish

Surface

terra-cotta pots size 8-inch (20 cm), 3-inch (7.5cm) and 2-inch (5cm), from any home goods or craft store or garden center

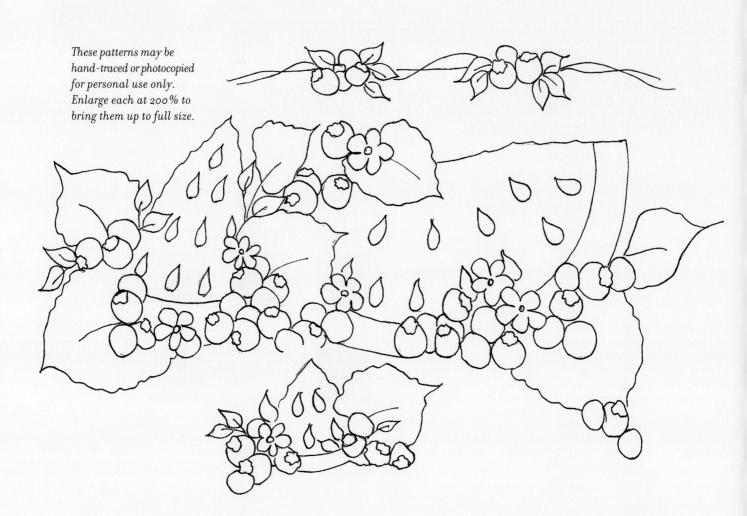

These patterns may be hand-traced or photocopied for personal use only. Enlarge each at 200% to bring them up to full size.

Watermelon

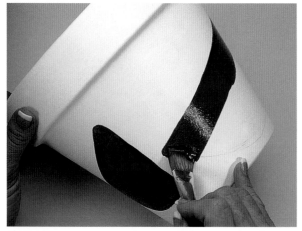

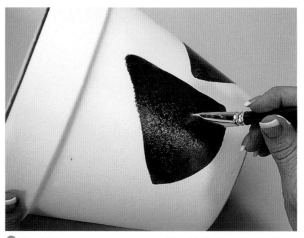

1 Basecoat the pots with Wicker White. Using your ¾-inch (19mm) flat, basecoat the watermelon shape with Engine Red side loaded with a little Berry Wine. Keep the Berry Wine to the outside edge of the watermelon shape.

2 Double load your medium scruffy with the same two colors. Pounce in for texture. Be sure to cover any brush lines from basecoating.

Rind, Leaves and Berries

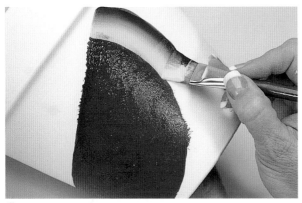

3 Double load your ¾-inch (19mm) flat with Yellow Light and Green Forest. Keeping the Yellow Light against the red, paint the rind following the shape of the melon.

4 Using the same brush and colors as you used for the rind, paint in the large leaves. Keep the green to the outside. Add the stem using the chisel edge of your brush.

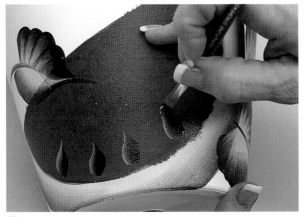

5 Load your no. 6 flat with Licorice. Side load with Wicker White and push, turn and lift to the chisel to form the teardrop-shaped watermelon seed.

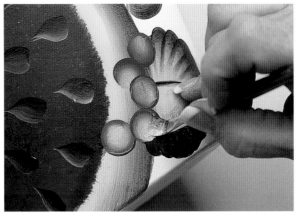

6 Double load your no. 6 flat with Night Sky and Wicker White, and stroke in the berries. First paint a half circle, keeping the white to the center.

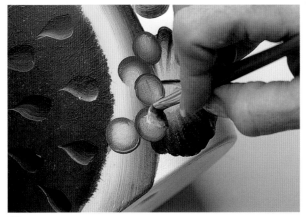

7 Flip the brush and finish the other side.

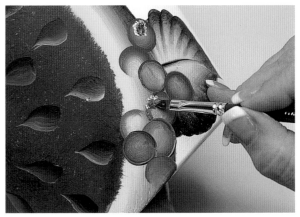

8 Touch in the blossom ends using your no. 2 flat with a lot of Night Sky, side loaded with a touch of Wicker White. Keep the Night Sky to the center.

Blossoms and Curlicues

9 *(Top Left)* Add the petals using your no. 6 flat double loaded with Yellow Light and Wicker White. Stroke in a little teardrop for each petal.

10 *(Top Right)* With Green Forest on the end of your brush, dot in the flower centers.

11 *(Left)* Add curlicues with inky Green Forest and your no. 2 script liner brush.

Border

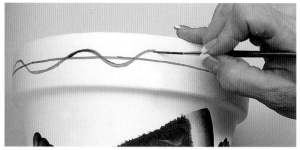

12 Use your no. 2 script liner with inky Green Forest to create the border. Keep the border the same distance all the way around the pot by running your little finger along the top edge of the pot as you paint the border.

13 Add the wavy liner throughout the border. Complete the border by adding berries, leaves and curlicues, according to the pattern (see final picture).

Napkin Rings

14 To create the napkin rings, turn the smallest pot upside down. Place the tip of a large drill bit into the hole and drill through it.

final step

Protect your flowerpots with several coats of water-based varnish. You must also seal the inside if you plan to use the pots for planting.

Daisy Mat

My husband and I have found a wonderful use for that extra piece of vinyl flooring you have tucked away in your basement or garage! Paint a cheery daisy mat for your porch or entryway.

This project uses big brushes and no pattern. I want you to create your own mat using whatever flowers and colors you choose.

The shape of your mat will be decided after you are finished painting since that is when you will cut out the shape.

Note: If you don't have any vinyl flooring, ask at any flooring store for leftover remnants. They may be happy to get rid of them, and the price could be next to nothing!

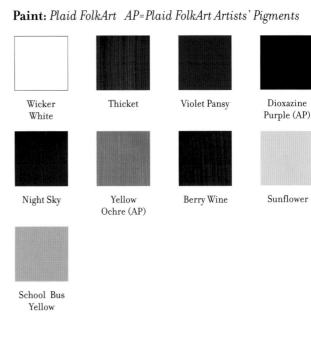

Paint: *Plaid FolkArt   AP=Plaid FolkArt Artists' Pigments*

Wicker White	Thicket	Violet Pansy	Dioxazine Purple (AP)
Night Sky	Yellow Ochre (AP)	Berry Wine	Sunflower
School Bus Yellow			

Brushes

1½-inch (38mm) flat ❖ no. 12 flat ❖ medium scruffy

Additional Supplies

scissors ❖ water-based exterior varnish

Surface

vinyl flooring remnant

Large Daisies and Pansy Bud

1 Paint the large daisies using a simple teardrop stroke. Load your 1½-inch (38mm) flat with School Bus Yellow and Wicker White. Form a teardrop shape by beginning on the chisel, pushing out, then lifting back up to the chisel.

2 Using the same teardrop stroke, layer the half daisy over the full daisy.

3 With Thicket, Wicker White, and School Bus Yellow on your medium scruffy brush, pounce in the center of your daisy.

4 Using your 1½-inch (38mm) flat multiloaded with Berry Wine, Wicker White, and School Bus Yellow, paint a pansy bud. Stroke in the first petal—push, wiggle, then slide back down to the end. For the second petal, just wiggle out and slide back.

5 For the third petal, touch, lean, then chisel down. If you choose to add a large pansy with these colors, follow the instructions for the pansies (steps 6 through 11).

Pansy

6 Double load your 1½-inch (38mm) flat with Night Sky and Wicker White. Keep the Night Sky to the outside, and paint the back pansy petals with a seashell stroke.

7 Repeat this stroke for the two side petals.

8 For the two bottom side petals, flip the brush over. Add School Bus Yellow to the light side of the brush, and continue the seashell stroke.

9 Make the two bottom petals with teardrop strokes. Keep Night Sky toward the outside edge of the petal.

10 Using your no. 12 flat with Thicket and School Bus Yellow, stroke in the center stamen using a chisel stroke.

11 Using Thicket on the handle of your brush, dot in the center of the flower.

Leaves and Lilacs

12 Paint in large heart-shaped leaves using your 1½-inch (38mm) flat double loaded with Thicket and Sunflower. With the chisel edge of your brush, paint in the stem, leading with the lighter color.

13 Use your medium scruffy brush with Violet Pansy, Dioxazine Purple, and Wicker White to pounce in the background for the lilacs.

14 Using your no. 12 flat, alternate picking up Violet Pansy, Wicker White, and Dioxazine Purple. Push down hard on the the chisel edge of your brush to stroke in the flower petals.

15 Use School Bus Yellow on the end of your brush to dot in the flower centers.

Finishing

16 Use your script liner and inky Thicket to loosely outline the flower petals.

17 With scissors or a craft knife, cut the vinyl following the outside shape of your painted mat.

final step

Protect your painted mat with several coats of water-based exterior varnish.

Herb and Insect Pots

Add beautiful pots to your garden with these quick and easy herb and insect pots. I love the little insects and the variety of flowers on this set of pots.

Make as many or as few of these as you want. They make wonderful gifts as sets, or place a candle in one or more and light up a summer evening. They can also hold an array of garden goodies.

Note: There are four different pots in this project. The colors for all four are shown at right, but the colors for each specific pot are listed preceding the individual instructions. Please refer back to this page if you need to see a particular color.

Paint: *Plaid FolkArt AP=Plaid FolkArt Artists' Pigments*

Italian Sage	Burnt Umber (AP)	Wicker White	Sunflower
Yellow Light (AP)	Yellow Ochre (AP)	Licorice	School Bus Yellow
Thicket	Engine Red	Night Sky	Berry Wine

Brushes

¾-inch (19 mm) flat ❖ no. 12 flat ❖ no. 6 flat ❖ no. 1 script liner ❖ no. 2 script liner ❖ medium scruffy

Additional Supplies

water-based exterior varnish

Surface

terra-cotta pots size 8-inch (20cm), 6-inch (15cm), 4-inch (10cm), 3-inch (7.5cm) and 2-inch (5cm) from any home goods or craft store or garden center

All Pots

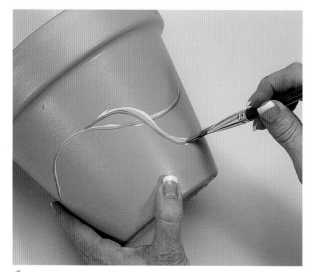

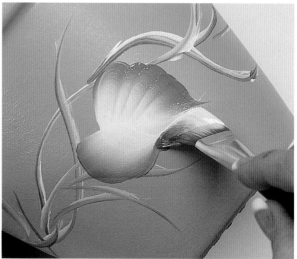

1 Basecoat the pots with two coats of Italian Sage. Transfer the patterns on to each pot. On all pots, paint in the vines first, using the largest brush with which you are comfortable. I used my ¾-inch (19mm) flat on the large pots and my no. 12 flat on the smaller ones. Using Burnt Umber, Wicker White and your flat, paint in the vines using the chisel edge of your brush, leading with the lighter color. Paint one vine all the way around the pot. Add more vines starting on the main vine and crossing over.

2 Using Thicket and Sunflower and occasionally picking up Burnt Umber on your ¾-inch (19mm) flat, paint in heart-shaped leaves. Keep the outer edge of the second half of this heart-shaped leaf smooth. Slide your brush to the tip, leading with the yellow. Add stems using the chisel edge of your brush. For all the smaller pots, use your no. 12 flat for the leaves.

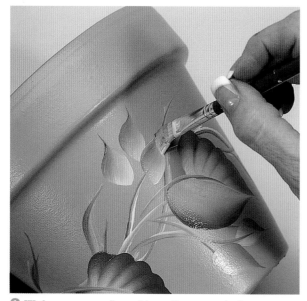

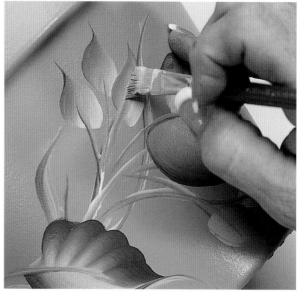

3 With your no. 12 flat, add small one-stroke leaves using Sunflower and Thicket.

4 Pull the stem halfway into the leaf using the chisel edge of your brush.

Bumblebee Pot

Colors:

❖ Thicket ❖ Sunflower
❖ Yellow Ochre (AP)
❖ Yellow Light (AP)
❖ Wicker White
❖ Burnt Umber (AP)

Brushes:

❖ no. 12 flat ❖ no. 6 flat
❖ no. 2 script liner

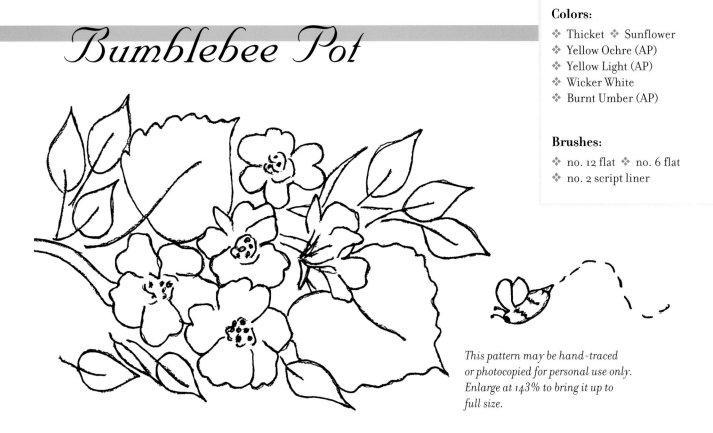

This pattern may be hand-traced or photocopied for personal use only. Enlarge at 143% to bring it up to full size.

5 *(Left)* Load your no. 12 flat with Wicker White, and side load with Yellow Light to stroke in the flower petals. Keep the yellow to the inside.

6 *(Right)* Using your no. 12 flat with Sunflower and Thicket, pull a stem from the bottom of your flower with the chisel edge of your brush.

7 *(Left)* Dot in the flower centers using Yellow Light on the handle of your brush. Using your liner with Thicket, scallop around the yellow center to accent.

8 *(Right)* Paint in curlicues with inky Thicket on your no. 2 script liner.

Bumblebee Pot, continued

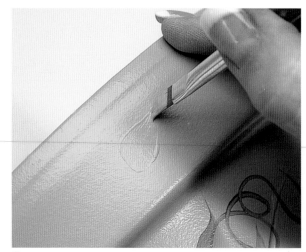

9 Use your no. 6 flat and Yellow Ochre to base in the bee's body with a push-turn-lift stroke. Just push down on the brush, turn, then lift up to the chisel edge to form the tail end of the bee.

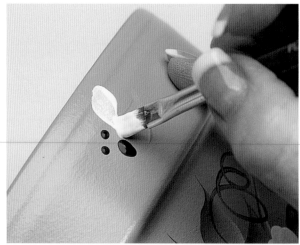

10 With the handle of your brush and Burnt Umber, dot in the head and antennae. Use your no. 6 flat and Wicker White to stroke in the wings. Push on the chisel edge of your brush, then lift as you come to the body. Make the second wing overlap the first wing.

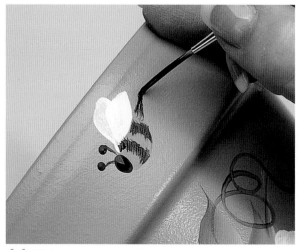

11 With your no. 2 script liner and Burnt Umber add the antennae ends to the head. Use short furry strokes to add the stripes on the bee.

12 Using the same brush with Burnt Umber, add the motion lines behind the bee

Butterfly Pot

This pattern may be hand-traced or photocopied for personal use only. Enlarge at 118% to bring it up to full size.

Colors:
- ❖ Burnt Umber (AP)
- ❖ Wicker White
- ❖ Berry Wine ❖ Night Sky

Brushes:
- ❖ no. 12 flat
- ❖ no. 2 script liner

13 *(Top Left)* Using your no. 12 flat double loaded with Berry Wine and Wicker White, paint in the petals on your pot. Make the first petal with a downward chisel stroke.

14 *(Top Right)* Make the second petal with a teardrop stroke: push out then finish up on the chisel. Repeat this stroke a few more times to make more petals.

15 *(Bottom Right)* Lightly touch the brush to the pot to leave a light trailing of flowers. Attach the stem to the flower as you did on the first pot.

Butterfly Pot, continued

16 Using your no. 12 flat double loaded with Night Sky and Wicker White, stroke in the top butterfly wing.

17 Stroke in the second wing the same way as you did for the top wing. Stroke in the bottom wings using only the chisel edge of your brush.

18 To form the body, load your no. 2 script liner with Burnt Umber, then just lay the bristles down to form the body.

19 Lift the brush and curve the body down as you lift.

20 Add the antennae as you did for the bumblebee. For the head, touch just the tip of the brush, then pull back.

Dragonfly Pot

Colors:

❖ Night Sky
❖ Yellow Light (AP)
❖ Wicker White ❖ Licorice

Brushes:

❖ no. 12 flat ❖ no. 6 flat
❖ no. 2 script liner

This pattern may be hand-traced or photocopied for personal use only. Enlarge at 111% to bring it up to full size.

21 *(Left)* With Night Sky and Wicker White on your no. 12 flat, paint in the asters. Use the chisel edge of your brush, leading with the white.

22 *(Right)* Dot in the centers with Yellow Light on the end of your brush.

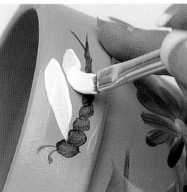

23 *(Left)* To form the dragonfly body, load your no. 6 flat with Licorice then push-lift, push-lift, on the chisel edge of your brush, all the way down. Use your no. 2 liner to paint in the tail.

24 *(Right)* Add the antennae. For the dragonfly wings, load Wicker White on your no. 6 flat, touch, push, then slide up to the chisel.

Colors:

- ❖ Engine Red ❖ Licorice
- ❖ Wicker White
- ❖ Burnt Umber (AP)
- ❖ Yellow Ochre (AP)

Brushes:

- ❖ no. 2 script liner
- ❖ medium scruffy

Ladybug Pot

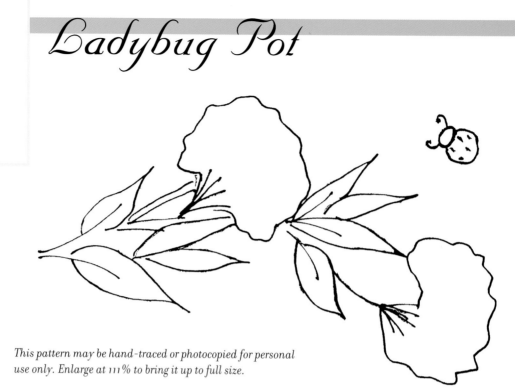

This pattern may be hand-traced or photocopied for personal use only. Enlarge at 111% to bring it up to full size.

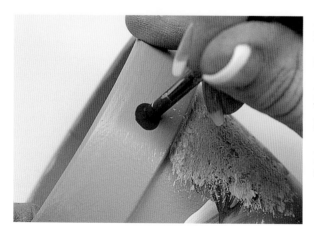

25 *(Top Left)* Use your no. 2 script liner with Burnt Umber and Wicker White to pull the cluster of little stems for the blossom.

26 *(Top Right)* Now use your medium scruffy brush with Wicker White and Yellow Ochre to pounce in the flower blossoms.

27 *(Bottom Left)* Dot in Engine Red with your brush handle, then spread this out into a small circle.

28 Add Licorice with a pencil tip or the end of a small brush handle to create the bug's head, the antennae dots and the dots on the body.

29 Use your no. 2 script liner and Licorice to finish the antennae and the center line on the ladybug.

final step

Protect the pots with a couple of coats of clear varnish.

Floral Garden Screen

I hope you find this enchanting garden screen as enjoyable to paint as I did. If you have a corner of your garden that needs some color, this screen will fulfill that purpose. At least these little visiting bunnies won't do any damage; they just want to hang out in the garden too.

When the weather turns cold, bring the screen indoors and use it as a fireplace screen.

Note: You will be using a comb fan brush in this project. The fan brush should always be used dry. If it gets too wet you won't be able to create the little hairs on the bunnies—the paint will run together and streak. So always dry the brush thoroughly on a paper towel before each use.

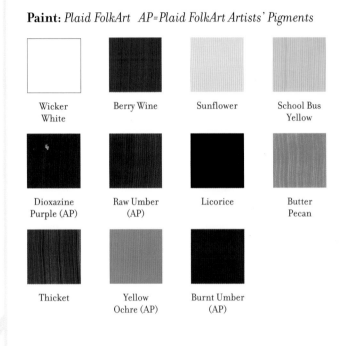

Paint: *Plaid FolkArt   AP=Plaid FolkArt Artists' Pigments*

Wicker White	Berry Wine	Sunflower	School Bus Yellow
Dioxazine Purple (AP)	Raw Umber (AP)	Licorice	Butter Pecan
Thicket	Yellow Ochre (AP)	Burnt Umber (AP)	

Brushes

1½-inch (38mm) flat ❖ 1-inch (25mm) flat ❖ ¾-inch (19mm) flat ❖ no. 12 flat ❖ no. 2 script liner ❖ no. 6 flat ❖ no. 6 comb fan ❖ large scruffy ❖ medium scruffy ❖ small scruffy

Additional Supplies

floating medium ❖ water-based exterior varnish

Surface

wooden cutout by Dewberry Designs

This pattern may be hand-traced or photocopied for personal use only. Enlarge first at 200%, then at 153% to bring it up to full size.

First Bunny

1 Basecoat your wood with two coats of Wicker White, and trace on the pattern. Use floating medium and your no. 12 flat double loaded with Butter Pecan and Raw Umber to stroke in the first bunny's ear. Keep the Raw Umber to the outside.

2 Quickly go into the wet paint with your no. 6 comb fan brush and pull little hairs from the inside to the outside of the ear.

3 With the same loaded no. 12 flat, use the Raw Umber edge to paint in the rest of the ear.

4 With Wicker White and Raw Umber on your no. 12 flat, chisel edge the white fur line along the ear.

5 Restroke that same part of the ear with your no. 12 flat. Float a little Raw Umber along the right edge and, while still wet, quickly use your no. 6 comb fan brush to create little hairs.

6 Paint the other ear in the same manner.

7 Double load your no. 12 flat with Raw Umber and Butter Pecan, and stroke in the base of the head. Keep Raw Umber to the outer edge and shape in the bunny's head.

8 Fill in the face using downward strokes, following the contour of the head.

First Bunny, continued

9 With your no. 12 flat, pick up Wicker White, Butter Pecan, Raw Umber, and floating medium. Again follow the shape of the bunny's head, keeping the darker color to the outside. Quickly pick up your no. 6 comb fan brush and, while the paint is still wet, pull out some hairs around the edge of the face.

10 Use the chisel edge of your no. 12 flat double loaded with Butter Pecan and Raw Umber to pull in the crease of the mouth. Lead with the lighter color.

11 Draw the shape of the nose with the Raw Umber edge of the brush.

12 Shade in above the nose with Raw Umber, using short upward strokes. Float a little Wicker White to define underneath the nose and around the bottom lower cheek.

13 Fill in the body with your no. 12 flat and a float of Butter Pecan.

14 Then, quickly pull the fur with your no. 6 comb fan brush. Pull some fur at the edge of the body to give him a fluffy appearance.

15 Using your no. 12 flat double loaded with Butter Pecan and Wicker White, lead with Butter Pecan and chisel edge some highlights into the fur.

16 Using the chisel edge of your brush, continue to pull the Raw Umber into the white right under the mouth.

Eyes

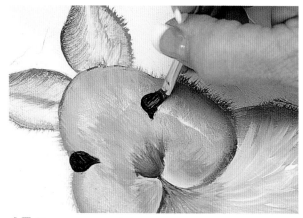

17 Using your no. 6 flat and Licorice, basecoat in the bunny's eyes.

18 Pick up Wicker White on the Licorice brush and, ever so lightly, shape the eyeball as shown.

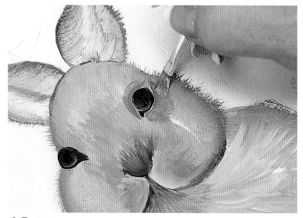

19 Add darker shading above and below the eyes with Raw Umber and a touch of Butter Pecan. This will add depth.

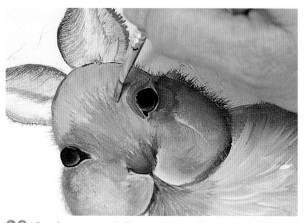

20 Load your no. 6 flat with Raw Umber and floating medium. Stay on the chisel edge and stroke in fur between the eyes.

21 Place some white highlights of fur under the eye using your no. 6 flat side loaded in Wicker White. Drag the white behind.

Ears and Whiskers

22 Outline the eyes still using your no. 6 flat with floating medium side loaded in Wicker White. Keep the white to the outside edge.

23 Use your no. 2 script liner and thick Wicker White to apply the highlight to the bunny's eyes.

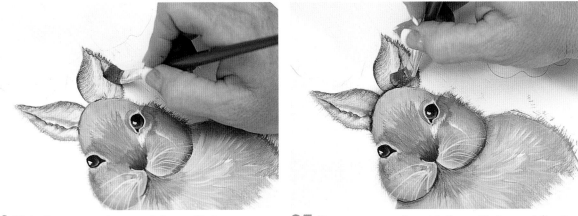

24 With floating medium and Burnt Umber on your no. 12 flat, follow the outline of the white fur to accent the depth of the inner ear.

25 Use your no. 12 flat with Burnt Umber and floating medium to shade underneath the neck, the top of the head and in front of the ears.

26 Use your no. 2 script liner and inky Wicker White to paint in the whiskers.

Leaves

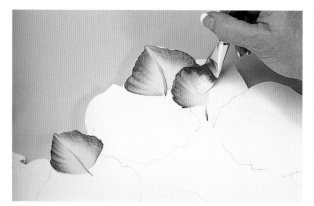

27 Begin stroking in large heart-shaped leaves using your 1-inch (25mm) flat loaded with Thicket, Sunflower, and Wicker White.

28 Stroke in the second half of the leaf using the same stroke.

29 Pull a stem into the center by using the chisel edge of your brush and leading with the white.

30 Softly stroke in shadow leaves in the background using your dirty 1-inch (25mm) flat with a lot of floating medium.

31 This is how your garden screen should look now.

Pink Irises

32 Finish filling in the shadow leaves, then begin painting the irises.

33 Using Sunflower, Wicker White, and Berry Wine on your 1-inch (25mm) flat, fill in the back petal of the iris. Start by wiggling up one side and lifting to a point.

34 Reverse the direction of the bristles, and wiggle back down to the other side. Keep the lighter edge to the outside.

35 For the two side petals, wiggle up and chisel down.

36 Layer the petals in the front, and add as many petals as you want using either of the previous two strokes.

Pink Irises, continued

37 *(Above)* For the lower petals, wiggle down and chisel back up to the base of the blossom.

38 *(Right)* Using the chisel edge of your brush with your leaf colors, pull down three or four short strokes beginning at the base of the blossom. Lean slightly on the chisel edge and pull a stem down.

Cabbage Roses

39 Using your 1-inch (25mm) flat double loaded with Berry Wine and Wicker White, paint in the back petals using a seashell stroke. Begin on the chisel edge with the white facing upward. Push down on the bristles, wiggle and then slide up to the chisel edge to finish the stroke.

40 Paint in the circled apron on the bottom, using the same seashell stroke.

41 Stroke in the back of the bud. Begin on the chisel edge, push up slightly and slide down, finishing on the chisel as shown.

Cabbage Roses, continued

42 The front of the center bud is a **U** stroke. Begin on the chisel edge, push down slightly and slide up to the chisel edge to finish.

43 Begin the second layer of petals where you just finished the bud. Use the same touch, push and wiggle (as you did in step 39) to create a seashell stroke. Keep the white facing outward.

44 Repeat this on the left side of the bud, still keeping the white facing outward.

45 This is how the rose looks after the second layer of petals is finished.

46 If you want to clean up the bud, just restroke the **U** stroke.

Cabbage Roses, continued

47 Start the filler petals on the right side. Chisel, keeping the white to the outside.

48 Continue the stroke, lifting the Berry Wine edge and dragging the bristles across the bud.

49 Repeat for the left side.

50 Chisel stroke another petal underneath the previous two petals to finish your rose. Complete all of the roses by repeating steps 39 to 50.

Irises

51 Using your 1-inch (25mm) flat triple loaded with Berry Wine, School Bus Yellow, and Wicker White, paint in the center irises following steps 33 through 38.

52 This is how your garden screen looks at this point.

53 Paint the purple irises in the same manner as the other irises, but change the color on the front petals.

Begin with the back petals and use your 1-inch (25mm) flat loaded with Dioxazine Purple, Wicker White and floating medium. Stroke in these petals by wiggling up to the top, changing directions and wiggling back down. Keep the white facing outward. Use the same stroke you used to paint the previous irises.

54 To form the two side petals, wiggle out and chisel back toward the flower center.

Irises, continued

55 Add School Bus Yellow to the white corner of your 1-inch (25mm) flat, and stroke in the center front petals as you did the back petals.

56 Stroke in the two side front petals using a downward wiggle stroke, then chisel back up.

57 With Thicket and Sunflower on your no. 12 flat, chisel in the stem, leading with Sunflower.

58 Use your no. 12 flat double loaded with Thicket and School Bus Yellow to chisel in the stamen wherever you like. Lead with the Thicket and drag the yellow behind.

59 Add the foliage at the bottom by multiloading your large scruffy with Thicket, Sunflower, and Wicker White. Pounce to fill in the base of the screen.

Second Bunny

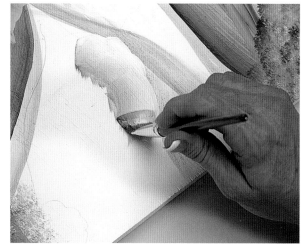

60 Begin the second bunny at the back ear. Basecoat with Raw Umber and Wicker White on your ³/₄-inch (19mm) flat. While the paint is still wet, pull hairs with your no. 6 comb fan brush. Fill in the ears as you did for the first bunny; continue to stroke then pull fur.

61 Reload your ³/₄-inch (19mm) flat with more Wicker White, and paint in the chest area. Stroke along the back, then fill in the body using the same brush.

63 Add floating medium to the Raw Umber, and stroke along the top edge.

62 Paint the arm with the dark edge of the brush (the Raw Umber side), drawing the shape of the arm.

Second Bunny, continued

64 Take the no. 6 comb fan brush, and pull hairs into the arm and down onto the body a little bit.

65 Using your ³⁄₄-inch (19mm) flat loaded with Raw Umber, Wicker White and floating medium, stroke the outer shape of the head, then fill in. Pull the stroke in to the head slightly to form the nose (see photo for step 66).

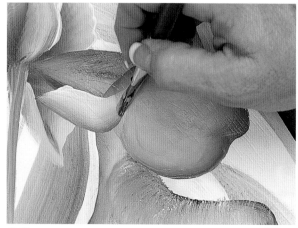

66 Stroke the bottom part of the front ear with the same dirty brush.

67 Chisel stroke the top section of the ear.

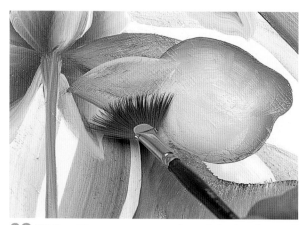

68 While still wet, use your no. 6 comb fan brush to pull hairs from the top section down into the bottom section.

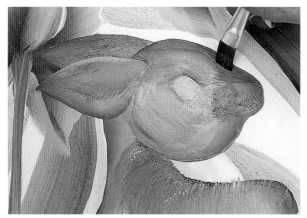

69 Use Raw Umber and floating medium on your no. 12 flat to float shading on the head and above the nose. Also dab around the whisker area using the same brush.

70 Paint in the eye using the same colors and techniques as you used for the first bunny (see steps 17 through 26). Outline the nose and the eye with Wicker White side loaded with floating medium on your no. 6 flat.

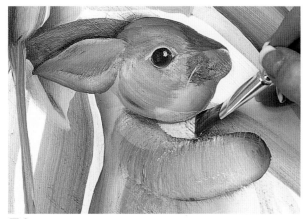

71 Using your ³⁄₄-inch (19 mm) flat with floating medium and Burnt Umber, float shadows around the head and ears to make the bunny stand out from the background.

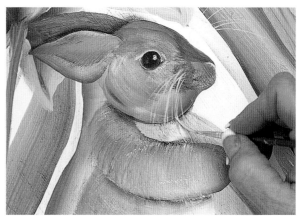

72 Pull whiskers with inky Wicker White on your no. 2 script liner.

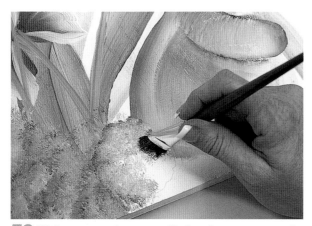

73 With your medium scruffy brush, pounce on the bunny's tail using Raw Umber and Wicker White.

Pansies

74 Paint the purple pansy using Dioxazine Purple and Wicker White on your ¾-inch (19mm) flat. Use a seashell stroke, keeping the purple facing outward. For the lower petals, pick up School Bus Yellow on the white side of the brush. Beginning on the chisel edge, push down and out with your brush and slide up to the end, still keeping the purple to the outside.

75 Begin the pink pansy using School Bus Yellow and Berry Wine. For the back petal keep the Berry Wine to the outside. Pick up Wicker White and floating medium. Form the two seashell-shaped petals with the white on the outside edges.

76 Paint the lower petals on each side, picking up a little more School Bus Yellow.

77 Pick up a lot of Berry Wine and School Bus Yellow, and paint the two teardrop petals at the bottom.

78 With your no. 12 flat loaded with School Bus Yellow and Thicket, paint the center using a downward chisel stroke. Dot the center with School Bus Yellow on the handle of your brush.

Butterfly and Bumblebee

79 Paint the butterfly with Dioxazine Purple and Wicker White. Paint the body with inky Thicket on your no. 2 script liner. (See page 58 for butterfly instructions.)

80 Paint the bumblebee with Yellow Ochre on your no. 12 flat. Paint the stripes and head with your no. 2 script liner using Licorice. Use your no. 6 flat with Wicker White to paint the wings. (See page 56 for bumblebee instructions.)

final step

Use several coats of water-based exterior varnish on your floral garden screen to protect it from the elements.

Hydrangea Bench

My almost three-year-old grandson has discovered that gardening with Grandma is fun. I had this small version of my favorite garden bench constructed just so he felt that he, too, had a special place in the garden. This little bench will look pretty in a cozy corner of your garden.

Note: The grapevines on the sides of the bench base do not have a pattern; they are painted in a freehand style similar to the vine on the back of the bench.

Paint: *Plaid FolkArt   AP=Plaid FolkArt Artists' Pigments*

Wicker White

Thicket

Raw Umber (AP)

Berry Wine

Sunflower

Brushes

1-inch (25mm) flat ❖ ¾-inch (19mm) flat ❖ no. 12 flat ❖ no. 2 script liner ❖ large scruffy brush

Additional Supplies

floating medium ❖ water-based exterior varnish

Surface

small bench by Dewberry Designs

*These patterns may be hand-
traced or photocopied for personal
use only. Enlarge them first at
200%, then again at 200% to
bring them up to full size.*

Grapevines

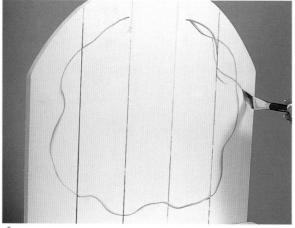

1 Prime the wood and allow it to dry, then basecoat the bench with Wicker White. With your 1-inch (25mm) flat double loaded with Wicker White and Raw Umber, add a placement stroke. Use the chisel edge of your brush, leading with the white, then intermingle the vine in and out to get the grapevine shape.

2 In the same manner, add vines to each side of the base of the bench to make a full grapevine. This is simply an X-shaped vine.

Bird's Nest and Large Leaves

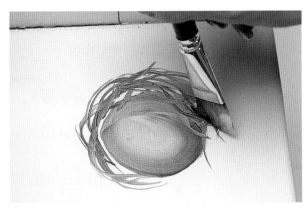

3 Next, basecoat the area for the bird's nest with Raw Umber and a touch of Wicker White. Use the same chisel-edged stroke to create the vinelike sides to the nest, just like in steps 1 and 2.

4 Over the basecoated area, paint the eggs using your no. 12 flat with Wicker White. Stroke in the two bottom eggs, then stroke in the top egg. Stroking over the based-in area gives shading to the egg.

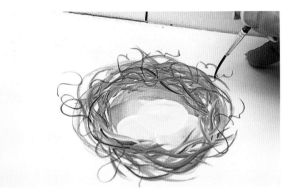

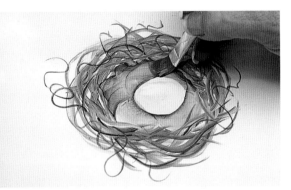

5 Use your no. 2 script liner with inky Raw Umber, and add some small curlicue vines around the nest.

6 Use floating medium and Raw Umber with your no. 12 flat to shade in depth on the inside of the nest. Then, shade around the eggs.

7 Use lots of floating medium with Wicker White, Thicket, and a small bit of Sunflower to stroke in the large heart-shaped leaves. Pick up a touch of Raw Umber every once in a while for variation. Add a lot of floating medium to some leaves and less to other leaves. Fill in all of your large leaves first.

8 Use your 1-inch (25mm) flat with the same colors to paint in some large one-stroke leaves.

Turned Leaf and Hydrangeas

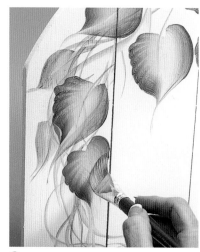  

9 With the same brush and colors, start the turned side of the leaf.

10 Flip the edge of the brush inward so that the darker green will be on the inside of the turned leaf edge.

11 Completely pivot the green edge of the brush around, slide, then end on the chisel edge. If you want the flipped edge to be more defined, add more paint to your brush, and restroke it.

12 *(Top Left)* With your ¾-inch (19mm) flat and a mixture of floating medium, a little Raw Umber, Wicker White, and Berry Wine, stroke in the bow shape. (See page 12 for ribbon stroke.)

13 *(Top Right)* Take your large scruffy brush with a little Raw Umber, Wicker White, and Thicket, and pounce in a background under the hydrangea. Pounce in one area on the seat for the hydrangea you will be painting there.

14 *(Bottom Left)* Double load your no. 12 flat with Wicker White and Raw Umber. Then, as you come forward, begin picking up Berry Wine on the Raw Umber side of the brush, and stroke in the petals of the hydrangea. Add more Berry Wine as you come forward, picking up a little Thicket now and then for more shading.

Finishing Touches

15 Add curlicues with inky Raw Umber on your no. 2 script liner. Dot the centers of the flowers with Sunflower on your brush end.

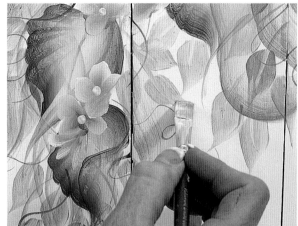

16 Add the shadow leaves using floating medium on your dirty no. 12 flat brush.

17 With Thicket, Wicker White, floating medium and a touch of Sunflower, use the chisel edge of your 1-inch (25mm) flat to add the stem on the bench seat. Add the little stems and fill in the hydrangea just as you did on the back of the bench (see steps 13 and 14).

18 Add small shadow leaves and curlicues on both sides of the bench base throughout the grapevine.

final step

Protect your bench with several coats of water-based exterior varnish.

Painted Trash Can

Wait until your trash collector sees this can! Trash isn't pretty, but this will help to dress it up a bit. If you don't want to use it for trash, it would be a great container for your gardening utensils, or even your dog's food.

Painting on metal is one of my favorite things to do. It's so quick and easy. Just remember not to mix any water with your paint; use only floating medium on metal surfaces. The faster you paint, the better metal painting will look.

Note: When painting on metal, be sure to prepare the surface by wiping it with rubbing alcohol first. If you are painting on a dry, basecoated metal surface (which you will be on the trash can base), be sure to have plenty of paint double loaded on your brush. Make each stroke definite so you will not have to restroke; restroking may pick up the basecoating. If this starts to happen, spray a light coat of sealer over the basecoat. Allow it to dry, and try again.

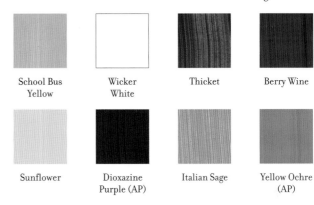

Paint: *Plaid FolkArt AP=Plaid FolkArt Artists' Pigments*

School Bus Yellow	Wicker White	Thicket	Berry Wine
Sunflower	Dioxazine Purple (AP)	Italian Sage	Yellow Ochre (AP)

Brushes

1-inch (25mm) flat ❖ no. 12 flat ❖ no. 2 script liner ❖ small scruffy ❖ large scruffy

Additional Supplies

rubbing alcohol ❖ water-based exterior varnish

Surface

metal trash can with lid from any home goods or hardware store

Background and Large Flowers

1 This is another in the book that does not require a pattern. I encourage freehand painting, and this project has such simple flowers that I feel certain you can create your own design with very little trouble. Feel free to change the colors or to borrow flowers, leaves or even insects from other projects in the book.

Wipe the metal surface with rubbing alcohol. Begin painting the trash can lid. With your large scruffy brush, pounce in the background for the flowers, using Wicker White, Sunflower, and Thicket. Go ahead and pounce in the background on the bottom of the can also.

2 For the side view of the yellow blossom, use your 1-inch (25mm) flat with Berry Wine, School Bus Yellow, and Wicker White. Push down, wiggle up and down and then chisel down to end the stroke. Keep the yellow to the outside.

3 For the full yellow blossom, paint five or more petals. To make these petals, start on the chisel, push down and wiggle.

4 Slide down to end the stroke. All of the flowers on this can are simply variations of the same three colors we used for the can lid: Berry Wine, School Bus Yellow and Wicker White.

5 For brighter yellow flowers use Yellow Ochre, School Bus Yellow, and Wicker White. Keep the yellow to the center. Double load your no. 12 flat with Berry Wine and School Bus Yellow, and chisel edge some outward strokes for depth in the center of the flower.

6 With your small scruffy brush, pounce in the center of the white flower using Yellow Ochre, a touch of School Bus Yellow, and Wicker White. For the center of the yellow flower, add Berry Wine to your scruffy.

Leaves and Butterflies

7 *(Left)* Use your liner and inky Thicket to outline the centers of the flowers with loose lines.

8 *(Right)* With your 1-inch (25mm) flat loaded with Thicket and Sunflower, chisel in stems, leading with the Sunflower.

9 *(Left)* Paint large leaves using your 1-inch (25mm) flat loaded with Sunflower and Thicket.

10 *(Right)* Now add the butterflies. Use Dioxazine Purple and Wicker White on your no. 12 brush for the wings on your butterfly. Paint in the body with your no. 2 script liner and Thicket.

Bottom of Can

11 *(Left)* Load Wicker White, Sunflower, and Thicket on your 1-inch (25mm) flat. Paint in the background stems, leading with the Sunflower. Beginning at the center stem, stroke in more stems that are bent over. Add leaves to them.

12 *(Right)* To make the back-facing flower darker, load your brush with mostly Berry Wine and just a touch of Wicker White.

For the rest of the blossoms start with the top petal and work down. With School Bus Yellow and Thicket on your liner, add the underneath stem and the stem on the back of the flowers.

Finish the blossoms and flowers as you did on the top. Remember to alternate the colors to get a variation in the flowers. Add the leaves as you did on the lid.

Hummingbird

13 With your no. 12 flat double loaded with Wicker White and Thicket, paint in the head. This stroke is a half circle.

14 Stroke in the hummingbird using a long, one-stroke leaf stroke. The green edge of the brush forms the back of the hummingbird.

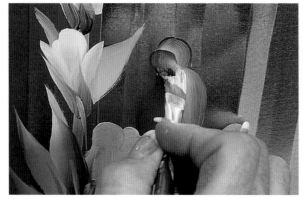

15 For the cheek, make a C-stroke inside the head area with Berry Wine and Wicker White on your no. 12 flat.

16 Continue the stroke all the way down the front of the body to form the bird's tummy. The Berry Wine edge of the brush forms the tummy.

17 Beginning right where the head touches the back, paint a one-stroke leaf shape to form the back wing of the hummingbird.

18 Using the chisel edge of your brush and leading with the white, chisel in feathers to the white edge of the wing, allowing the feathers to touch.

19 Still using Thicket and Wicker White, paint the front wing. Chisel edge the feathers all the way around the front of this wing. To keep the lines fine, stay on the chisel edge of your brush while pulling in.

20 Chisel edge in the tail feathers as you did around the wings. For the hummingbird eye, use your no. 2 script liner with Thicket and apply three little touch-pull strokes for the eye area. Add highlights with Wicker White. Add the beak with your liner, pulling the stroke out from the head. Now add the butterflies (see page 58 for detailed butterfly instructions).

final step

Protect your trash can with clear water-based varnish. Make sure the varnish is one that can be used on metal.

Garden Gate

This garden gate makes me think of an entrance to a secret garden. You can create this illusion by placing the gate in any area of your garden. Or place it inside of a trellis to enhance the entrance to your home.

Just follow the instructions to paint the hat and terra-cotta pots, add the one-stroke flowers, and you are ready to welcome your guests through your own garden gate.

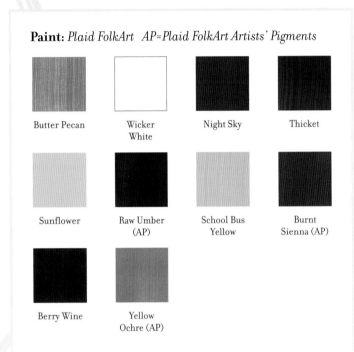

Paint: *Plaid FolkArt   AP=Plaid FolkArt Artists' Pigments*

Butter Pecan	Wicker White	Night Sky	Thicket
Sunflower	Raw Umber (AP)	School Bus Yellow	Burnt Sienna (AP)
Berry Wine	Yellow Ochre (AP)		

Brushes

1½-inch (38mm) flat ❖ ¾-inch (19mm) flat ❖ no. 12 flat ❖ no. 6 flat ❖ no. 2 script liner ❖ large scruffy

Additional Supplies

floating medium ❖ water-based exterior varnish

Surface

garden gate by Dewberry Designs

This pattern may be hand-traced or
photocopied for personal use only.
Enlarge at 200%, again at 200%, then
at 133% to bring it up to full size.

Straw Hat

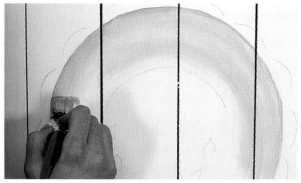

1 With Butter Pecan and floating medium on your 1½-inch (38mm) flat, stroke in the shape of the hat. Fill in the outer rim, then fill in the center of the cap in the same manner.

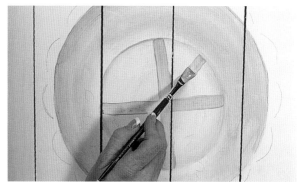

2 Load your no. 12 flat with Butter Pecan and floating medium. Crisscross the top of the hat to lay in the weave of the straw.

3 Once you have your crisscrosses in, you can begin weaving. Continue using your no. 12 flat with the Butter Pecan and floating medium. Pull your stroke around as if it were weaving under one, then stop. Go over the next one and stop. Just take your time.

4 For the next row, simply do the opposite—go over where you stopped and stop where you went over. You will begin to see a weave forming. If you ever need to clean up a mistake you can use a dampened paper towel.

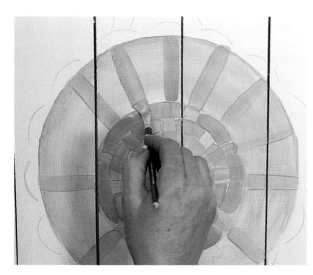

5 For the outer rim, continue the crisscross lines out to the outer edge.

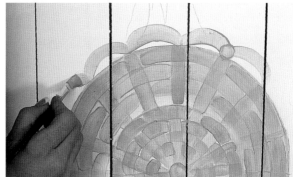

6 Still using Butter Pecan and floating medium, begin weaving over and under strokes as you did in the center. You will really begin seeing the definition at this point. Add the scalloped edge connecting the crisscross lines. Where each edge meets, paint a circle. To form the circle of the very center of the cap, stroke in a half circle, then flip your brush and make another half circle.

Ribbon

7 Load your no. 12 flat with Night Sky, Wicker White and floating medium. First pull the ribbon down to the hat, then add your loops up on top.

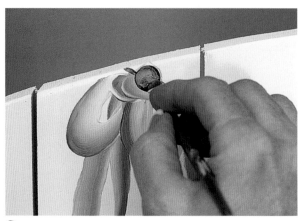

8 To form the nail head use your no. 6 flat with Butter Pecan and Raw Umber. Stroke in the nail head as you did the center circle of the cap.

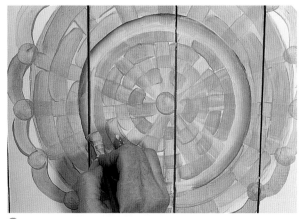

9 Use your no. 12 flat with Wicker White, Night Sky and floating medium to stroke in the ribbon around the center part of the hat. Keep the Night Sky to the outside of the ribbon.

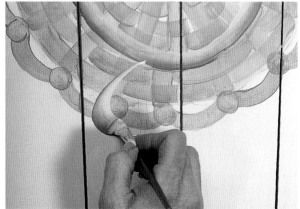

10 Stroke in the bow. Beginning on the chisel edge of your brush, start down the loop and push.

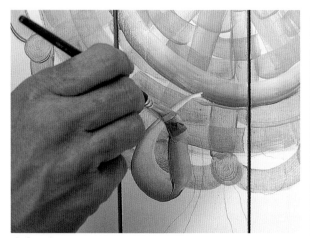

11 Flip the brush, push and end up on the chisel without stopping.

12 Finish with two of these on each side, then paint the trailing ribbon ends.

Flowers and Pots

13 Add the knot to the bow with two **C**-strokes. Using your no. 12 flat with Thicket and Sunflower, fill in around the ribbon with one-stroke leaves.

14 To add the flower buds and petals, double load your no. 12 flat with Yellow Ochre and Wicker White. Stroke them in as shown.

15 Paint the pink flowers using your no. 12 flat double loaded with Berry Wine and Sunflower. Finish off with curlicues using your no. 2 script liner with inky Thicket.

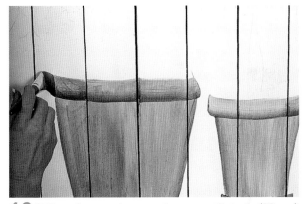

16 Fill in the pot shapes using your 1½-inch (38mm) flat loaded with Butter Pecan, floating medium and Burnt Sienna. Keep the Burnt Sienna to the outer edge. Paint the rim and base last.

17 Load your 1-inch (25mm) flat with Raw Umber and floating medium. Float this under the rim and down the sides of the pots.

Trunks, Foliage and Dragonfly

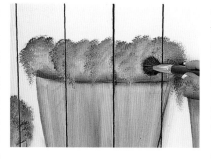

18 (*Left*) Use Raw Umber, Wicker White and your 1½-inch (38mm) flat to paint in the grapevine trunk. Use the chisel edge of your brush, and lead with the white.

19 (*Top Right*) Add moss to the top of each flowerpot.

20 (*Bottom Right*) Load your large scruffy brush with Thicket and Sunflower, occasionally picking up some Raw Umber. Add more moss draping over the top of the gate in several places.

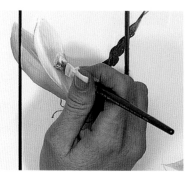

21 (*Left*) Use Thicket and a little Butter Pecan on your no. 12 flat to add one-stroke leaves. Pull stems in to connect the leaves. Add inky Thicket curlicues and an inky Berry Wine bow on the topiary with your no. 2 script liner.

22 (*Top Right*) Using your no. 12 flat double loaded with Thicket and Night Sky, paint in the dragonfly body (see page 59 for dragonfly instructions). Use Night Sky and your no. 2 script liner to add the legs. Use Wicker White and a touch of Night Sky with your no. 12 flat to add the wings.

23 (*Bottom Right*) Because the wings are so long you may need two strokes for each one.

Spider Plant, Flowers

24 On the chisel edge of your no. 12 flat double loaded with Wicker White and Thicket, pull the baby spider plant stems up and out from the moss. Still using the chisel edge of your brush, add leaves. Vary the thickness of the leaves by pushing and lifting; also vary the direction of the leaves. Be sure and keep them wispy looking. Add the spider babies. Take your liner and add some roots underneath each of these.

25 Using Sunflower, Wicker White, and Thicket on your ³⁄₄-inch (19mm) brush, paint stems for the flowers. Add the large ripple-edged leaves, keeping the lighter area to the inside of the leaf. Add the long skinny chisel-edged leaf. For the smaller ripple-edged and one-stroke leaves, use your no. 12 flat with Sunflower, Wicker White and Thicket.

26 Use your no. 12 flat double loaded with Berry Wine and Wicker White to stroke in the pink flowers. Keep the Berry Wine to the outer edge.

For the purple flower, use Night Sky and Wicker White. Keep the Night Sky to the outer edge. Start the blossoms at the top and work down the plant. Pull stems downward from the blossoms.

Using your no. 12 flat loaded with School Bus Yellow, Yellow Ochre, and Wicker White, stroke in the daisies using the chisel edge of your brush. Pounce in the daisy centers using your small scruffy loaded with Berry Wine and Yellow Ochre.

final step

Protect your garden gate with several coats of water-based exterior varnish.

103

Wedding Bells
Painted Pots

Can you tell I like clay pots? I think that's because they are so easy to find and just as easy to paint. They make great last-minute gifts and have so many uses.

These beautiful pots will be a wonderful accent to your next outdoor wedding celebration or anniversary party. Filled with rice, almonds or plants, or topped with votive candles, these pots with the simple elegant design of white wedding bells and pink roses will fit in easily with any wedding theme.

I have chosen the sentiment "for all time and eternity" for the small pots, but feel free to add whatever sentiment you would like to complement your own personal celebration.

Paint: *Plaid FolkArt*

Italian Sage

Wicker White

Metallic Rose

Sunflower

Thicket

Violet Pansy

Brushes

¾-inch (19mm) flat ❖ no. 12 flat ❖ no. 6 flat ❖ no. 2 flat ❖ no. 2 script liner

Additional Supplies

floating medium ❖ water-based exterior varnish

Surface

terra-cotta pots size 8-inch (20cm), 3-inch (7.5cm) and 2-inch (5cm) from any home goods or craft store or garden center

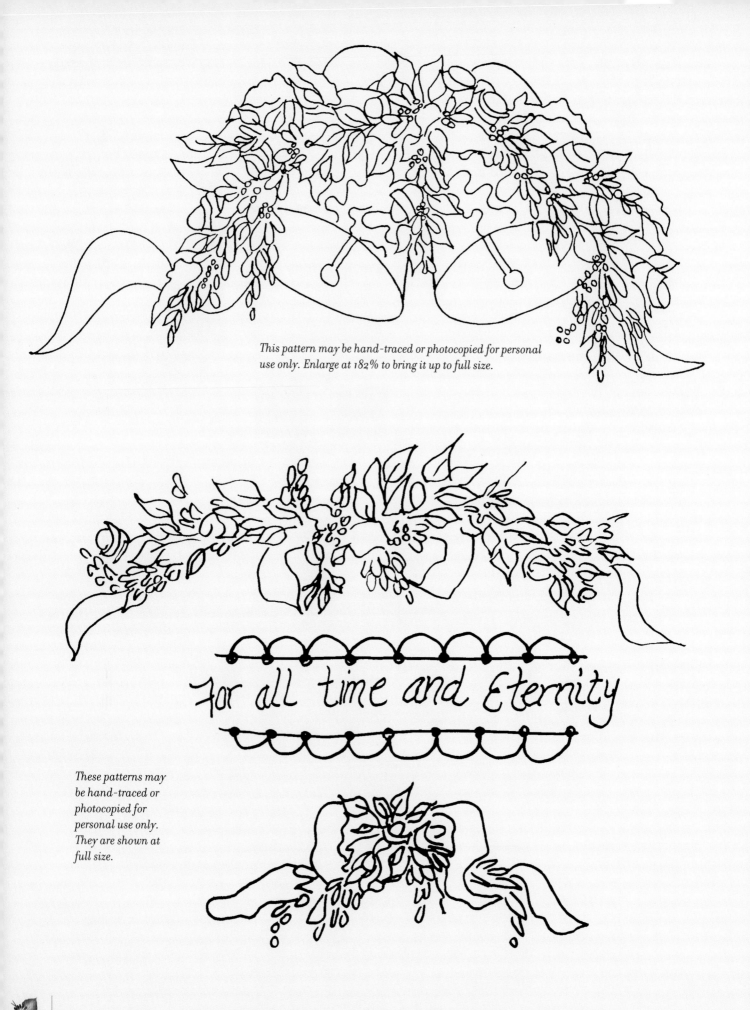

This pattern may be hand-traced or photocopied for personal use only. Enlarge at 182% to bring it up to full size.

For all time and Eternity

These patterns may be hand-traced or photocopied for personal use only. They are shown at full size.

Bells and Ribbon

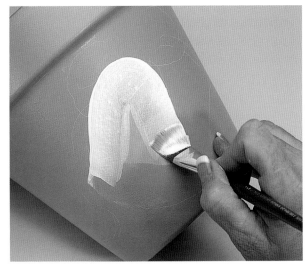

1 Basecoat the pots with Italian Sage. Double load floating medium and Wicker White onto your ¾-inch (19mm) flat. Outline the shape of the bells, and fill in the center using downward strokes.

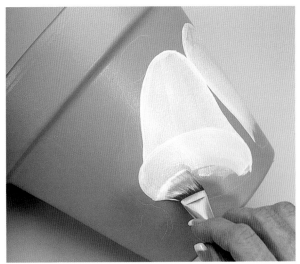

2 Pick up fresh Wicker White, and shape in the bottom of the bell. Just outline it and fill in, keeping the brush flat the whole time.

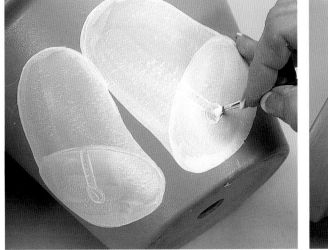

3 With your no. 2 flat and Wicker White, stroke in the ringer as shown.

4 Still using Wicker White and your ¾-inch (19mm) flat, add ribbon to the top of the bells. Use a chisel-push-chisel stroke.

Ribbon, continued

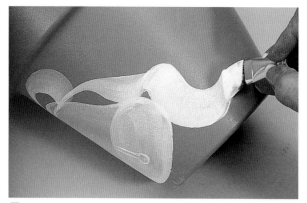

5 Create turns in your ribbon by pushing down, then pull back up to the chisel.

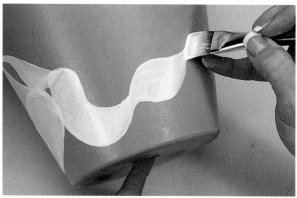

6 Push down once again, then pull back up to the chisel to end the ribbon.

7 Use your liner and thick Wicker White to outline your ribbon. This will make it look like wired ribbon.

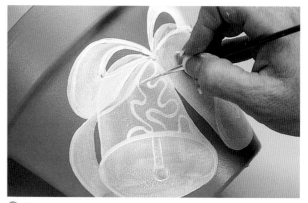

8 Using your liner with inky Wicker White, outline the lip of the bells in the same way. Add the lacy embossing effect to the sides of the bells.

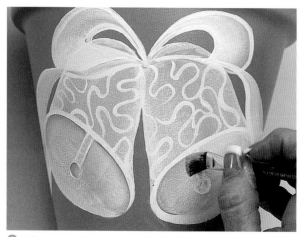

9 After the white is completely dry, use your no. 12 flat with Italian Sage and floating medium to shade in the depth under the bell. Also, float a little on the ball of the ringer to accent.

Rosebuds

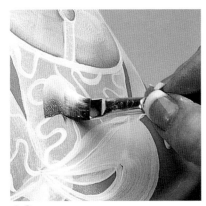
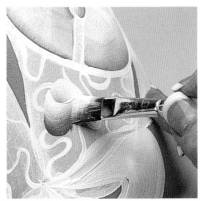
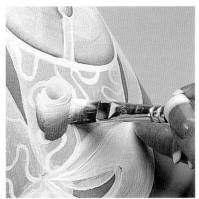

10 Turn the pot upside down. Using your no. 12 flat with Metallic Rose and Wicker White, stroke up and over to start the rosebud.

11 Now paint the U-shaped petal.

12 Pick up more Wicker White, and add two or three more strokes to create the layers of petals in front of the U-stroke. Add the other rosebuds in the same manner.

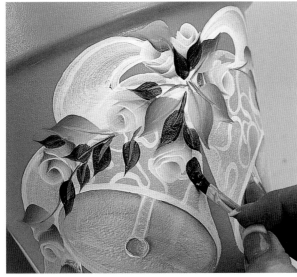

13 With your no. 12 double loaded with Sunflower and Thicket, add the larger leaves. Pull in the stems using the chisel edge of your brush and leading with the lighter color. Use straight Thicket on the no. 6 flat with floating medium, and paint in the darker leaves. Immediately pull in the stems using the chisel edge of your brush.

14 Add curlicues around the leaves with your no. 2 script liner and inky Thicket.

Trailing Blossoms and Ribbon

15 Double load Violet Pansy and Wicker White onto your no. 12 flat, and add the trailing blossom petals with a chisel-edge stroke. Lead with the purple and drag the white behind.

16 As you trail off, dab the tips of the bristles to make a natural look.

17 Add dots around the trailing blossoms with the end of your brush and Sunflower.

18 Load your ¾-inch (19mm) flat with Wicker White, and thin with a tiny bit of floating medium—enough to give it a sheer effect. Paint in the ribbon around the top edge of your pot. With your no. 2 script liner, outline the edges of the ribbon as you did in step 7.

Scalloped Edges

19 Still using Wicker White and your liner, add the scalloped edges. Add dots where the scallop meets the ribbon as you go around the edge.

final step

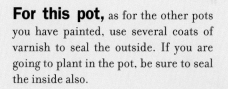

For this pot, as for the other pots you have painted, use several coats of varnish to seal the outside. If you are going to plant in the pot, be sure to seal the inside also.

Birdbath

Create an instant birdbath yourself with terra-cotta pots! Simply place one large pot upside-down and a second pot right-side-up on top of it. Add a large terra-cotta saucer, and there you have it.

A good thing about this birdbath is that it can easily be stored during those months that the birds are away. The birds don't seem to mind the portability of it as long as they can bathe in beauty.

Note: The birdbath can also be used as a table by simply adding a round glass tabletop to it. You can find the glass tops at any home goods or variety store that sells portable round end tables. Just measure the saucer to be sure the glass top will fit, overlapping by about an inch.

Paint: *Plaid FolkArt   AP=Plaid FolkArt Artists' Pigments*

Grass Green	Thicket	Engine Red	Wicker White
Licorice	School Bus Yellow	Berry Wine	Sunflower
Tapioca	Night Sky	Brilliant Ultramarine	Pure Orange (AP)
Yellow Light (AP)	Metallic Rose	Dioxazine Purple (AP)	Green Forest

Brushes

1-inch (25 mm) flat ❖ ¾-inch (19mm) flat ❖ no. 12 flat ❖ no. 2 script liner

Additional Supplies

One-Stroke sponges ❖ floating medium ❖ water-based exterior varnish

Surface

two 14-inch (35cm) terra-cotta pots, and one 20-inch (51cm) saucer from any home goods or craft store or garden center

These patterns may be hand-traced or photo-copied for personal use only. Enlarge them first at 200%, then at 172% to bring them up to full size.

Water and Lily Pad Leaves

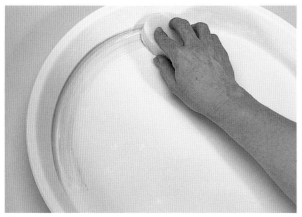

1 Basecoat both pots and the saucer with Tapioca. Using your One-Stroke sponge with Brilliant Ultramarine, Wicker White and floating medium, paint around the outer edge of the saucer for your waterline.

2 Finish filling in the center with a circular motion.

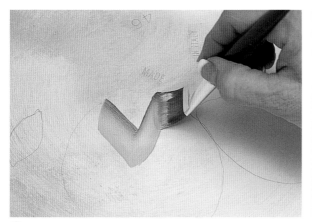

3 Using your 1-inch (25mm) flat, double load Grass Green and Thicket and add a touch of floating medium. Begin the leaf by making a **V** shape on the water.

4 Follow around the outer edge of the leaf, keeping the darker green to the outside. Continue filling in the center, then paint the second leaf in the same way.

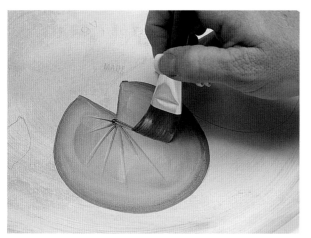

5 Dab on a touch of Thicket at the base of the V with the end of your brush. Using your dirty brush, pull veins from this spot into the leaf, leading with the lighter side. Repeat for the second leaf.

Pink Blossom

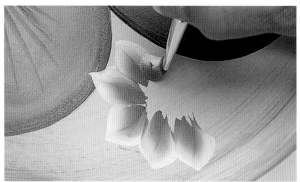

6 Double load your no. 12 flat with Wicker White and Metallic Rose. Stroke in the flower petals. Keep the white to the outer edge, and stroke up to the chisel.

7 Pull the stroke down to the other side. Continue these strokes around in a circle to form the outer layer of petals.

8 Repeat for a second and third layer, staggering the petals.

9 Paint the bud by layering three of these petals on top of each other.

10 Use your no. 2 script liner to paint in the flower center with Yellow Light and Pure Orange. Touch and pull out, alternating between the two colors.

11 Still using your script liner and thick Wicker White, touch on the stamens. Add leaves to your bud with Grass Green and Thicket.

Goldfish

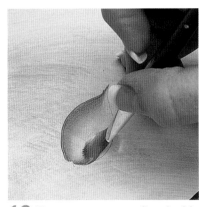  

12 Using your no. 12 flat double loaded with Pure Orange and Yellow Light, outline the shape of the fish. Keep the Yellow Light inward while filling in the body.

13 For the top fin, pull a stroke down to the body and overlap it with a second shorter stroke.

14 Pick up some Wicker White, and touch the bottom of the tail, push and lift to a point. Repeat this for the second side of the tail.

15 Take the white edge of the brush, outline the edge of the tail fin, then pull back in toward the body. Repeat for the second side of the tail.

16 Pick up more Wicker White on your brush. Using the chisel edge, stroke upward to form the bottom fins.

Goldfish and Water Ripples

17 Side load more Pure Orange onto your no. 12 flat, and restroke the body of the fish to clean up the edges.

18 Side load some more Pure Orange to paint the gill.

19 Add Pure Orange to your no. 2 script liner, and touch in the mouth. Crisscross lines of inky Pure Orange for the scales on the fish's body.

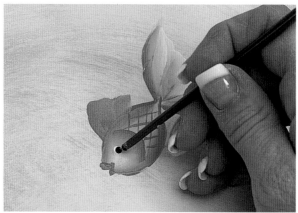

20 With Wicker White on the end of your brush, dot in the eyes. Make sure this white is completely dry, then go in and add a smaller dot of Licorice with the end of your brush. Add a touch of Wicker White highlight on each eye with the liner. Repeat steps 12 through 20 to paint the second goldfish.

21 Before you proceed with this step, make sure that everything is completely dry. Load your 1-inch (25mm) flat brush with floating medium and side load into the Wicker White. Paint in the water ripples over the goldfish (take care not to get any on the leaves).

Foliage

22 *(Left)* Stack the pots as shown, and work on both at the same time. With a touch of Thicket, Grass Green and lots of floating medium on your 1-inch (25mm) flat, start at the bottom and stroke upward to paint in some shadow ferns for the background.

23 *(Top Right)* With Wicker White and Thicket on your 1-inch (25mm) flat, loosely base in some ground area for the background shading.

24 *(Left)* With the same mixture on your ³/₄-inch (19mm) flat, add the stem of the fern. Use your no. 12 brush with Thicket and Grass Green for the fronds. Beginning at the top of the stem, pull long leaves, gradually make these longer as you go down the fern. Occasionally cross leaves over each other for a more natural look.

25 *(Top Right)* Restroke the stem using the two greens and your no. 12 flat brush.

Mushrooms

26 Using your no. 12 flat with Wicker White and a touch of Licorice, paint in the mushroom stems. Use your 1-inch (25mm) flat with Yellow Light and Engine Red to basecoat in the red mushroom top on the right side. For the center red mushroom, use Engine Red. Base in the red and orange mushroom on the left with Yellow Light and Pure Orange. Grab a little Engine Red on your brush, and pull the Engine Red into the wet top cap color, beginning at the bottom edge. With Wicker White and Licorice on the no. 12 flat, add the underneath of the middle red mushroom cap using a downward stroke on the chisel edge of your brush.

27 To add the skirt to the white mushroom and the far right mushroom, use Wicker White and Licorice. Lay your no. 12 flat down flat and wiggle it as you stroke upward.

28 Basecoat the top of the white mushroom using your 1-inch (25mm) flat double loaded with Wicker White and Licorice. Keep the white toward the top. For the bottom edge, hold the Licorice toward the bottom edge and wiggle for a ruffled effect. To emphasize the ruffling, use floating medium and Licorice to stroke in some dark creases.

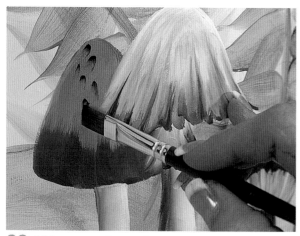

29 Add spots to the mushroom with floating medium and Licorice on your no. 12 flat. Paint upside-down U-strokes ever so lightly to create the spots.

30 With floating medium and Licorice or Thicket, shade in a little edge under each mushroom cap.

Irises and Bluebells

31 On the darker mushrooms, add the spots with floating medium and Wicker White, making U-shapes. Add grass with Thicket and Sunflower on the chisel edge of the no. 12 flat, stroking from the bottom up.

32 There are two irises located behind the mushrooms. Use Dioxazine Purple and Wicker White on your ³/₄-inch (19mm) flat for the top three petals and add Yellow Light to your brush for the front two bottom petals. (Follow the instructions for the irises on page 73 and 74.) Add the leaves using Thicket with a touch of Green Forest.

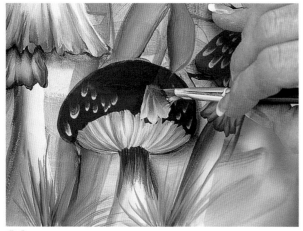

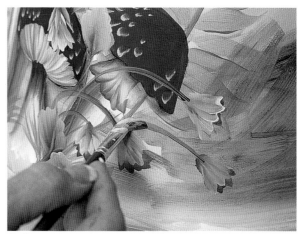

33 Using Night Sky and Wicker White and your no. 12 flat brush, stroke in the bluebells. Start at the backside of the blossom and ripple the bottom edge. Keep the darker color facing the bottom edge. Add more white to your brush, and form little points on the front side of the blossom.

34 Use your no. 12 flat brush with Thicket and Sunflower to add the stems, calyxes, then the leaves.

Daisies

35 Now add the daisies. The stroke for all of the daisy petals is touch, lean and lift on the chisel of your no. 12 flat as you pull to the center. Add the yellow daisies using Yellow Light, Pure Orange, and Wicker White. Put a generous amount of paint on your brush, and alternate colors for variety. Use Wicker White and Engine Red for the red daisies.

36 Apply some Yellow Light to the centers. Begin in the center, and chisel the yellow out from the center into each petal. Use your no. 2 script liner, and dot the center of the daisies with Thicket.

37 With inky Green Forest, add fine stems pulled from the bottom of the blossoms.

38 Add leaves using Yellow Light and Green Forest on your no. 12 flat. Pull stems into the leaves to finish.

Dragonfly

39 To form the body of the dragonfly, use your no. 12 flat with Night Sky and Green Forest, and push-lift, push-lift. Apply less pressure as you go down the body.

40 Use your no. 2 script liner and Night Sky to touch and pull for the antennae. Use inky Night Sky for the tail. Pull away from the body.

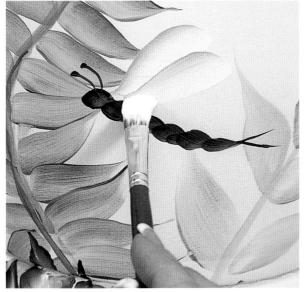

41 To paint the wings, load your no. 12 flat with Wicker White and just a touch of Licorice to get a gray tone on one edge of your brush. Begin the stroke away from the body and push and lift to the chisel edge, ending at the body.

42 Overlap the second wing on top of the first. Add two smaller wings underneath the larger ones.

Butterfly, Leaves and Flowers

43 Use School Bus Yellow and Wicker White with just a touch of Pure Orange on your no. 12 flat to stroke in the butterfly wings. Push and lift to the chisel edge. Add the body using a push-pull stroke with your liner and Thicket.

44 Basecoat the leaves using your ³/₄-inch (19mm) flat. Use Thicket and Sunflower with a little floating medium to fill in the background leaves. Add the front leaves using your no. 12 flat loaded with Green Forest and Sunflower.

45 Add the pink wildflowers using your no. 12 flat brush with Berry Wine and Wicker White. Overlap petals to form a circle. Slide out, wiggle and slide back in. Keep the white to the outer edge of each petal.

46 Pull down the top bud using downward chisel strokes.

47 With School Bus Yellow on the end of your brush, add the yellow dots in the center.

Final Touches

48 Add the leaves with Thicket and your no. 6 flat brush. Finish by pulling stems halfway into each leaf.

49 Add the leaves on the front edge using your 1-inch (25mm) flat with Thicket and Sunflower. Flip the brush back and forth while crisscrossing.

final step

Protect your birdbath with several coats of water-based exterior varnish.

Gazing Ball & Watering Can

Two must-haves for every garden are a gazing ball and watering can. With these implements you will have the essentials for gardening—at least my style of gardening. I like to water my flowers and then, more than anything, to simply sit and gaze into the past and future all at the same time.

I love the big beautiful hibiscus blossom on these bright metal surfaces, and I think you will be pleased with how simple these flowers are to paint. There's no pattern needed—just freehand the flowers and leaves wherever you'd like them.

Note: Remember, before painting on metal, clean the surface with rubbing alcohol, and be sure to not add water to your paint.

Paint: *Plaid FolkArt   AP=Plaid FolkArt Artists' Pigments*

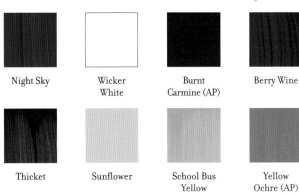

| Night Sky | Wicker White | Burnt Carmine (AP) | Berry Wine |
| Thicket | Sunflower | School Bus Yellow | Yellow Ochre (AP) |

Brushes

Watering Can
1-inch (25 mm) flat ❖ ³/₄-inch (19 mm) flat ❖ no. 12 flat ❖ no. 2 script liner ❖ small scruffy

Gazing Ball
³/₄-inch (19 mm) flat ❖ no. 12 flat ❖ no. 2 script liner ❖ small scruffy

Additional Supplies

rubbing alcohol ❖ water-based exterior varnish

Surface

galvanized metal watering can, 8-inch (20cm) glass gazing ball from any garden supply store

Watering Can

1 Clean the metal surface with rubbing alcohol. Use your 1-inch (25 mm) flat double loaded with Thicket and Sunflower to chisel in vines around the can.

2 Still using the same brush and the same colors, add large heart-shaped leaves. Keep the Sunflower toward the middle. Pull stems into the leaves using the chisel edge of your brush.

3 Using your no. 12 flat with the same two colors, add little one-stroke leaves and pull stems into them.

4 Using your ¾-inch (19mm) flat double loaded with Night Sky and Wicker White, paint in the large hibiscus blossom. To paint a petal, slide up on the chisel edge, leading with the white, and wiggle up.

5 After you've wiggled up, slide partially back down.

hint

If you let your strokes dry while painting on metal, you will lift up the paint underneath— it's better to paint wet-on-wet when painting on metal.

6 Wiggle up again and slide back all the way down.

7 Repeat these steps for the other four petals. Notice that on one of the lower petals if you turn your brush a little on the chisel, it flips the petal edge.

8 Using the chisel edge of your brush, pull Burnt Carmine into the wet blue center (make sure it's wet).

9 Use your no. 12 flat with School Bus Yellow and Thicket and add the stamen to the center of the flower. Pull up on the chisel edge.

10 Load your small scruffy with School Bus Yellow, Sunflower and a touch of Wicker White. Pounce in the fuzzy part on the stamen.

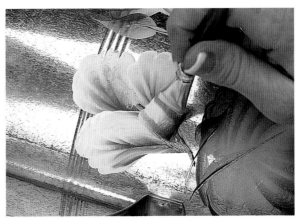

11 For the turned flower, paint in back petals first, then stroke in your stamen.

12 Then stroke the last petal right on top.

13 With Night Sky, Wicker White and your ¾-inch (19mm) flat, push the white with the chisel and stroke in the hibiscus bud.

14 Overlap this stroke with a second stroke.

15 Add the calyx to the bud and the unopened blossom using Thicket and Sunflower. Add one-stroke leaves.

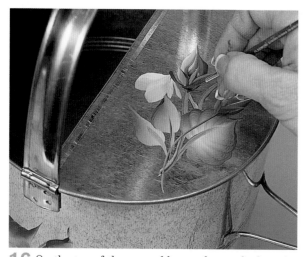

16 On the top of the can, add some leaves, buds and a butterfly. For the butterfly's wings, use School Bus Yellow and Wicker White on the ¾-inch (19mm) flat. Use Thicket on the no. 2 script liner for the body (see page 58).

Gazing Ball

17 Clean the surface with rubbing alcohol. Using Thicket and Sunflower on your ¾-inch (19mm) flat brush, begin the gazing ball as you did the watering can. On the chisel edge of your brush, chisel in a vine. With the same brush and colors, add large leaves. With your no. 12 flat, add the smaller one-stroke leaves, pulling the stems to them.

18 Use your ¾-inch (19mm) flat with Night Sky and Wicker White to paint in the large hibiscus blossom. Add the Burnt Carmine center and the yellow stamen.

19 Finish with the butterfly, following the steps for the watering can.

final step

Protect the surface with several coats of clear varnish that is made for metal.

Topiary Bench

Topiaries are so much easier to paint than they are to grow—at least the ones I have attempted to grow in the past. In addition to the topiaries on this bench, there's one more bunny for you to paint as well.

I bet you will often find yourself drawn to this bench to relax. What a wonderful place to spend any part of a summer day.

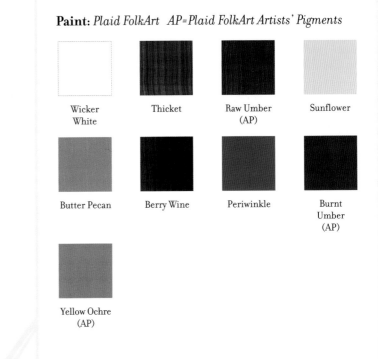

Paint: *Plaid FolkArt   AP=Plaid FolkArt Artists' Pigments*

Wicker White   Thicket   Raw Umber (AP)   Sunflower

Butter Pecan   Berry Wine   Periwinkle   Burnt Umber (AP)

Yellow Ochre (AP)

Brushes

1-inch (25mm) flat ❖ ¾ inch (19mm) flat ❖ no. 12 flat ❖ no. 6 flat ❖ no. 2 script liner ❖ large scruffy

Additional Supplies

One-Stroke painter's sponge ❖ floating medium ❖ water-based exterior varnish

Surface

wooden bench by Dewberry Designs

This pattern may be hand-traced or photocopied for personal use only. Enlarge first at 200%, then at 143% to bring it up to full size.

Sides of Bench

1 Prime all wood and allow it to dry, then basecoat in Wicker White. Trace on the pattern. Basecoat the pot with Wicker White and a little Butter Pecan. Continue to pick up Butter Pecan using your One-Stroke painter's sponge.

2 With your large scruffy brush and Thicket and Sunflower, pounce in the foliage. Don't pounce it too much or it will become one color. You want to see the different shades.

3 Load your no. 12 flat with floating medium, Butter Pecan and Raw Umber. Add the sculptured swag to the pot with one-stroke leaf strokes.

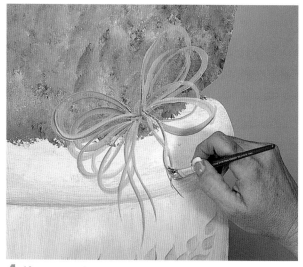

4 Alternating between Yellow Ochre, Butter Pecan, Raw Umber, and Wicker White, use your no. 12 flat and paint the raffia bow. Use the chisel edge of your brush.

Bench Back

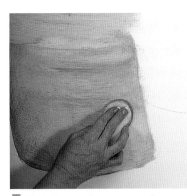

5 With Butter Pecan on a dampened sponge, basecoat in the three dark pots.

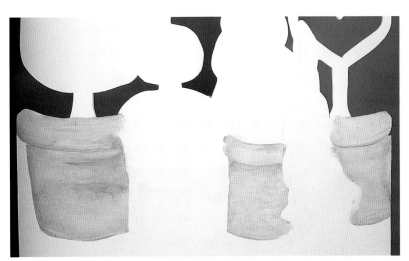

6 This is how your bench back should look now.

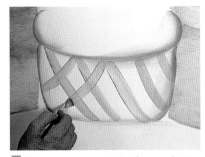

7 Using your 1-inch (25mm) flat double loaded with Raw Umber and Wicker White, paint in the shape of the lightest pot. Keep the Raw Umber to the outside. Add the crisscrossed lattice using your no. 12 flat with Butter Pecan and floating medium. Crisscross one way, then go back and cross over in the other direction.

8 Still using your no. 12 flat with floating medium and Raw Umber, shade in all of the details.

9 Add the leaf sculpture shapes on the right pot and the rose sculpture design on the left pot.

Branches and Bunny

10 Load Butter Pecan, Raw Umber, and Wicker White on your 1-inch (25 mm) flat. With the brush on the chisel edge, lead with the white, and add the trunks and branches. Be sure to continue the branches past where the foliage would begin; you will be covering this area up with green. If you stop short, the white background could show.

11 With your large scruffy brush loaded with Thicket, Sunflower, and Wicker White, pounce in the foliage. Keep the edges of the bunny clean as you pounce. You can clean this up with the sponge if needed. To create the layered effect on the foliage to the left of the bunny, layer from the bottom up, dark to light on each layer. Keep the darker topiaries in the back. For the front topiaries, use more Thicket with Wicker White for color variation.

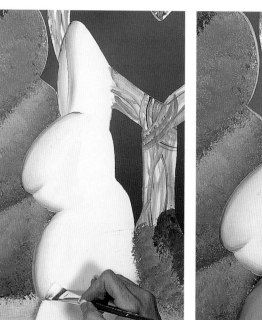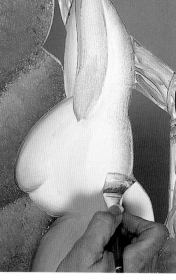

12 *(Left)* Begin with the back ear (which is on the left side), using your ³/₄-inch (19mm) flat double loaded with Raw Umber and Wicker White. Outline the front of the head and face, and follow down the front of the body to the top of the tummy.

13 *(Right)* Now outline the front ear, adding a very light touch of Berry Wine to the shading inside the ear (make sure to use a light touch). With Raw Umber and Wicker White, carry the outline down the back of the bunny head.

Bunny, continued

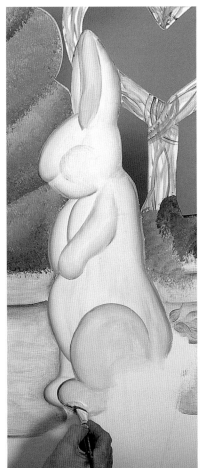

14 *(Left)* Follow the pattern, outlining the back arm and back leg first. Add the tummy, then add the front arm and the front leg. Fill in the front leg and arm with just a touch of Raw Umber. You should have white in there, and the Raw Umber should easily blend. Also add the cheek shape.

15 *(Below)* Add the bunny nose using the same colors and brush as in the last step. With your large scruffy brush, Raw Umber and Wicker White, pounce in the fluffy tail. Load your 1-inch (25mm) flat with Raw Umber and floating medium. Shade around your bunny—around his nose, arms and in front of and behind the bunny. Divide the topiaries a little by shading where they meet. Also shade under the moss.

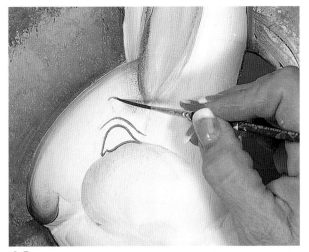

16 Use your no. 2 script liner to outline the eye, the crease, and the eyebrow using inky Raw Umber.

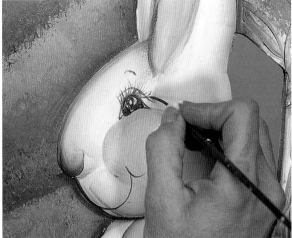

17 Add the mouth with inky Raw Umber on the no. 2 script liner. Still using your liner brush, use thick Raw Umber to dab in the eye. Add some Wicker White highlights. With Raw Umber, add eyelashes.

Rosebuds, Leaves and Butterfly

18 *(Top Left)* Use your no. 12 flat loaded with Raw Umber and Wicker White on the chisel edge of your brush to paint the bird's nest. Use Periwinkle and Wicker White to add the eggs. (See pages 86-87 for instructions for the bird's nest.) Add a few more curly vines using your liner and inky Raw Umber.

19 *(Top Right)* Using Wicker White, Berry Wine and floating medium on your no. 12 flat, stroke in the rosebuds (see page 32). Add the leaves beneath the rosebuds using your no. 12 flat double loaded with Thicket and Sunflower. Add a touch of Berry Wine.

Using your no. 12 flat with Thicket, Wicker White, and a touch of Raw Umber once in a while, add one-stroke leaves to the center section, over the bunny and over the pot on the right.

Add a butterfly near your rosebuds using Periwinkle and Wicker White for the wings and Thicket for the body (see page 58).

20 *(Bottom Left)* On the heart-shaped cutout, add a ribbon using your no. 6 flat with Berry Wine and Wicker White.

Finishing

21 Add the white petals over the topiary using your no. 12 flat, alternating with Wicker White, Sunflower and Yellow Ochre. Dot Thicket and Sunflower into the center with your brush handle.

On the heart, pounce in some wisteria with Wicker White and Periwinkle using your small scruffy brush. Also, add some wisteria to the front of the bunny.

Add rosebuds to the front of the bunny, and paint in the pink ribbon with Berry Wine and Wicker White on your no. 2 script liner.

With Periwinkle and Wicker White, stroke in six-petal flowers over the roses and ribbon.

Add curlicues with your liner and inky Thicket.

22 Antique the seat of the bench with Butter Pecan on a dampened sponge. Pounce moss in the corners and draping over the edge of the bench with Thicket, Sunflower, and Butter Pecan using your large scruffy brush.

final step

Spray your bench with several coats of a water-based exterior varnish.

Resources

PAINTS, MEDIUMS AND BRUSHES

Plaid Enterprises
3225 Westech Drive
Norcross, GA 30092
Phone (678) 291-8100
FAX (678) 291-8156
www.plaidonline.com

SURFACES

Boulder Hill Woodworks
HC 61 Box 1036
St. George, ME 04857
Phone (800) 448-4891
FAX (207) 273-6105

Dewberry Designs
124 Robin Road Suite 1700
Altamonte Springs, FL 32701
Phone (407) 339-0239
FAX (407) 339-5513
E-mail: dewberry@magicnet.com
www.onestroke.com

RETAILERS IN CANADA

Crafts Canada
2745 Twenty-ninth St. NE
Calgary, Alberta T1Y 7B5

Folk Art Enterprises
P.O. Box 1088
Ridgetown, Ontario N0P 2C0
Phone: (888) 214-0062

MacPherson Craft Wholesale
83 Queen St. E.
P.O. Box 1870
St. Mary's, Ontario N4X 1C2
Phone: (519) 284-1741

Maureen McNaughton Enterprises
RR #2
Belwood, Ontario N0B 1J0
Phone: (519) 843-5648

Mercury Art & Craft Supershop
332 Wellington St.
London, Ontario N6C 4P7
Phone: (519) 434-1636

Town & Country Folk Art Supplies
93 Green Lane
Thornhill, Ontario L3T 6K6
Phone: (905) 882-0199

RETAILERS IN UNITED KINGDOM

Art Express
Index House
70 Burley Road
Leeds LS3 1JX
Tel: 0800 731 4185
www.artexpress.co.uk

Crafts World (head office only)
No 8 North Street, Guildford
Surrey GU1 4AF
Tel: 07000 757070
Telephone for local store

Chroma Colour Products
Unit 5 Pilton Estate
Pitlake
Croydon CR0 3RA
Tel: 020 8688 1991
www.chromacolour.com

Green & Stone
259 King's Road
London SW3 5EL
Tel: 020 7352 0837
greenandstone@enterprise.net

Hobbycrafts (head office only)
River Court
Southern Sector
Bournemouth International Airport
Christchurch
Dorset BH23 6SE
Tel: 0800 272387 freephone
Telephone for local store

Homecrafts Direct
PO Box 38
Leicester LE1 9BU
Tel: 0116 251 3139
Mail order service

Index

B
Baby's breath, 39
Brushes, 8-9
    flat brushes, 8
    script liners, 9
    scruffy brushes, 8
Bumblebee, 56
Bunnies, 66-71, 79-81
Butterfly, 20

C
Colors, alternating, 13
Curlicues, 13

D
Daisies, 39
Double loading, 10
Dragonfly, 59

F
Ferns, 17-18
Flat brushes, 8
Flowers, 26-27
    baby's breath, 39
    daisies, 39
    hydrangea, 33-35
    irises, 73-74
    pansies, 48-49
    rosebuds, 32
    roses, 75-76
    water lilies, 115
Fruit, 42-43

G
Garden Gate, 96-104
Goldfish, 117-118
Grapevines, 86

H
Heart-shaped leaf, 12
Hummingbird, 94-95
Hydrangea, 33-35

I
Irises, 73-74

L
Lady bugs, 21
Leaves, 12-13
    heart-shaped leaf, 12
    shadow leaf, 13
    tall leaf, 12

M
Multiloading, 11
Mushrooms, 120

N
Nest, 87

P
Paint, 9
Pansies, 48-49
Pattern-tracing, 11
Plaid FolkArt Artists' Pigments, 9
Plaid FolkArt Floating Medium, 9
Plaid FolkArt Paint, 9
Projects
    Birdbath, 112-125
    Daisy Mat, 46-52
    Floral Garden Screen, 62-83
    Garden Gate, 96-104
    Gazing Ball & Watering Can, 126-131
    Herb and Insect Pots, 52-61
    Herb Barrel Stave, 22-27
    Hydrangea Bench, 84-89
    Mailbox Cutout, 28-35
    Painted Trash Can, 90-96
    Stepping-Stones, 14-21
    Topiary Bench, 132-141
    Watermelon Pot, 40-45
    Wedding Bells Painted Pots, 104-111
    White Flower Pot, 36-39

R
Ribbons, 12
Rosebuds, 32
Roses, 74-76

S
Script liners, 9
Scruffy brushes, 8
Shadow leaf, 13
Side loading, 11
Snails, 21
Starter strokes, 11
Stems, 12
Stepping-Stones, 14-21

Supplies, 8-13
    brushes, 8-9
    flat brushes, 8
    medium, 9
    paint, 9
    script liners, 9
    scruffy brushes, 8
Surfaces
    glass gazing ball, 127
    metal trash can, 91
    metal watering can, 127
    pressure-treated lumber stepping
        stones, 15
    terra cotta pot, 37, 41, 53, 105, 113
    vinyl flooring remnant, 47
    wood barrel stave, 23
    wood bench, 85, 133
    wood garden gate, 97
    wood garden screen, 63
    wood mailbox cutout, 29

T
Tall leaf, 12
Techniques
    colors, alternating, 13
    curlicues, 13
    double loading, 10
    multiloading, 11
    pattern-tracing, 11
    side loading, 11
    starter strokes, 11
    tracing the pattern, 11
Tracing the pattern, 11

V
Vines, 54

W
Water lilies, 115

More Decorative Painting Titles
from North Light Books

Start with an old or unfinished piece of furniture, add in a little acrylic paint and Kerry Trout's clever motifs, and you've got the makings of a handpainted masterpiece! This book provides 9 step-by-step projects that cover everything from preparing your surface to giving each piece an authentic, antique look.

ISBN 0-89134-980-4
paperback, 128 pages
#31539-K

Now you can capture the colors and textures of all your favorite fruits and berries, including lemons, strawberries, pears, plums, blackberries, apples, holly, pine sprigs and mistletoe. Priscilla Hauser provides 9 fully illustrated, step-by-step projects that teach you how to paint them on tin canisters, mini wheelbarrows and more!

ISBN 1-58180-070-3
paperback, 128 pages
#31684-K

This guide makes using color simple. Best of all, it's as fun as it is instructional, featuring 10 step-by-step projects that illustrate color principles in action. As you paint your favorite subjects—be they flowers, fruit or birds—you'll learn how to make color work for you.

ISBN 1-58180-048-7
paperback, 128 pages
#31796-K

Take your decorative painting to an exciting new level of depth and dimension by creating the illusion of reality— one that transforms your work from good to extraordinary! Patti DeRenzo, CDA, provides a complete course in the basic techniques of realistic painting, plus 6 exciting step-by-step projects.

ISBN 0-89134-995-2
paperback, 128 pages
#31661-K

These books and other fine North Light titles are available from your local art & craft retailer, bookstore, online supplier or by calling 1-800-289-0963.